Cheap Outboards

Cheap Outboards

The Beginner's Guide to Making an Old Motor Run Forever

Max E. Wawrzyniak III

BREAKAWAY BOOKS
HALCOTTSVILLE, NEW YORK
2006

Cheap Outboards: The Beginner's Guide to Making an Old
Motor Run Forever

ISBN: 978-1-891369-62-9
Library of Congress Control Number: 2005938238

Much of this book was originally published in the online
boatbuilding magazine, Duckworks.
www.duckworksmagazine.com

Published by Breakaway Books
P.O. Box 24
Halcottsville, NY 12438
(800) 548-4348
www.breakawaybooks.com

FIRST PRINTING JUNE 2006
SECOND PRINTING MARCH 2009
THIRD PRINTING JULY 2014

ACKNOWLEDGMENTS

I am indebted to many who have helped me
with old outboards in general, and with this
book in particular.

A few individuals deserve special mention,
however: Chuck Leinweber of www.duck
worksmagazine.com and small craft designer
Jim Michalak, who both promoted the project;
Bryant Owen of Ontario and Rob Rohde-Szudy
of Wisconsin who reviewed the manuscript; and
Garth Battista of Breakaway Books who
thought enough of the book to publish it. And
of course my wife who lets me play with my
toys and who helped with the manuscript.

Lastly, I would like to thank my parents,
who introduced me to boats (some powered by
outboard motors) almost upon the instant of
my birth, thereby setting my life on a course
that has never taken me far from the water. For
that I will always be truly grateful.

Contents

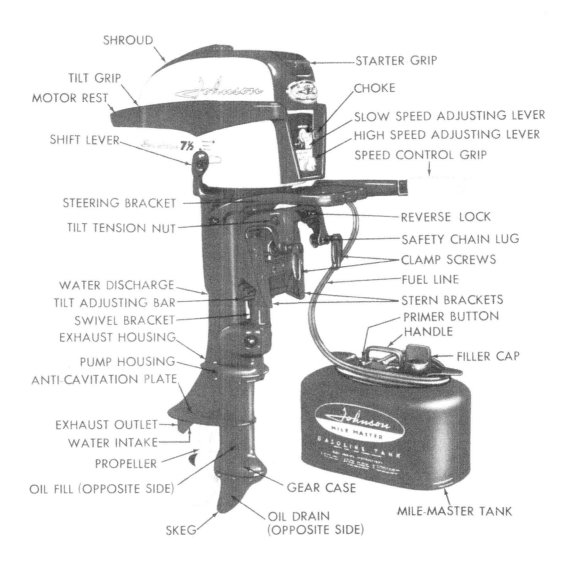

SHROUD

STARTER GRIP

TILT GRIP

MOTOR REST

CHOKE

SLOW SPEED ADJUSTING LEVER

HIGH SPEED ADJUSTING LEVER

SHIFT LEVER

SPEED CONTROL GRIP

STEERING BRACKET

TILT TENSION NUT

REVERSE LOCK

SAFETY CHAIN LUG

CLAMP SCREWS

WATER DISCHARGE

TILT ADJUSTING BAR

SWIVEL BRACKET

EXHAUST HOUSING

FUEL LINE

STERN BRACKETS

PRIMER BUTTON

HANDLE

PUMP HOUSING

ANTI-CAVITATION PLATE

FILLER CAP

EXHAUST OUTLET

WATER INTAKE

PROPELLER

OIL FILL (OPPOSITE SIDE)

GEAR CASE

MILE-MASTER TANK

SKEG

OIL DRAIN
(OPPOSITE SIDE)

The basic components of an outboard. This engine uses a remote fuel tank ("Mile-Master") that supplies fuel to the outboard through a rubber hose. Small outboards are often fitted with gravity-feed fuel tanks mounted directly on the engine. Shown here in tiller-control format, this model is easily converted to remote controls.

Preface

The anticipated reader of this book would rather own a shiny, new, 4-cycle outboard motor than a greasy, dented old one, all things being equal. But all is not equal and that shiny, new outboard will cost a chunk of change. And so you, the reader, have picked up this book to see if there is an alternative way to power your boat without emptying your bank account.

An old outboard motor (and I do mean *old*; maybe as old as fifty years) may provide you with a reliable power source for your boat for considerably less money than a new outboard or even a used late model one. But it has to be the right brand, the right model, and in the right condition. The right condition in this case means mechanically sound but not necessarily pretty. It is assumed that, as a "cheap outboard" seeker, you have more interest in fishing, skiing, or cruising than in collecting outboard motors. Yes, there really are people out there who collect old outboard motors, just as people collect stamps and Pez candy dispensers and watch fobs. But don't dismiss the collectors altogether, as these guys can be a big help in your finding the "right" old outboard and in getting it into running condition.

There are other "old outboard motor" books out there but these are primarily intended for the collector. This one is intended for the guy who wants to go boating for as little money as possible. This book is not a service manual; it is not intended to show how to make every repair. It is intended to be a supplement to a service manual, providing more detail on simple repairs. It is also intended to be a buyer's guide, advising the avoidance of engines requiring major repairs and engines for which replacement parts are difficult to find. There are a couple of other books that I will mention in Chapter 3 that will aid you in identifying the appropriate (in my opinion) engine to buy and I believe that by being selective as to the condition, you can acquire an old outboard that does not require you to perform repairs beyond the level of what would be considered maintenance or "light" repairs.

Figure 0.01
A 1960 Johnson 10 HP, rescued from a corner of a dark basement, provides economical power for this 14 foot aluminum semi-vee boat, for not much more money than the sales tax on a new 4-cycle outboard.

So the goal of this book is not to teach you how to overhaul an outboard, but rather to teach you how to buy an outboard that requires a "tune-up" rather than an overhaul, and to then instruct you on how to do the tune-up, with a bit more information than the service manuals provide. This book also covers some areas that a normal service manual might not cover, such as installing remote controls, converting a remote control engine to tiller control, converting a "pressure tank" motor to fuel pump use, and how to install a lanyard-equipped safety "kill switch."

Figure 0.02
A 1957 Johnson 18 HP outboard repaired and restored by the owner and mounted on his home-built 11 foot boat

The primary subject matter of this book is outboards of no more than 40 HP for a couple of reasons; the vast majority of outboards sold (even new ones today) are of no more than 40 HP, and because way back in the "old days" 40 HP was just about the biggest outboard available, depending upon the exact year of course. The other reason is that outboards of over 40 HP and with more than two cylinders start to get complicated and more difficult to work on. Since electric starting was common only in the largest of these old outboards, and battery

charging systems are extremely rare (the buyer sometimes did not get battery charging just because he got electric start; often it was an option), these items will not be covered by this book. Even the electric start versions of these old outboards were fitted with recoil starters for manual starting, and utilized magneto ignition which does not require a battery. Personally, I would get the engine running first, and then worry about the electric start later.

I will assume that you know nothing about repairing outboard motors. I do not believe that mechanics are "born." Mechanical ability, as I see it, is the capacity to look at a problem and to logically determine a solution. There are untold millions of people finding solutions to complicated issues everyday, yet for some reason many of these people feel themselves unqualified to try to repair engines, including outboard motors. And that is true in the case of modern outboards, which require specialized training in high-tech ignition and fuel delivery systems. But we are not going to discuss modern outboards here. Instead we are going to discuss outboards manufactured from the mid 1950s to the early 1970s, before the advent of electronic ignition and fuel injection. The 2-cycle (also known as "2-stroke") engines of this period are just about the simplest engines ever built, and performing minor repairs to engines of this period requires only a modest collection of tools and a minimum knowledge of mechanics. You probably already own most of the tools that you will need; this book is an attempt to provide you with some of the knowledge.

I am not a professional mechanic, nor have I

ever had any formal training in outboard repair. I have never been paid money to work on someone else's engines (although numerous "friends" have expected me to work on their outboards for free): my own collection of over a hundred old outboard motors affords me plenty of opportunity to mess with engines without the risk of upsetting a customer. This book has been written by someone who knew nothing about the subject until jumping into it with both feet. I have made a bunch of mistakes along the way and continue to make a few every now and then but I have learned a lot from my mistakes and from the mistakes of others and hope that I can save you from making some of the same ones. The methods and procedures detailed in this book have worked for me but I must make the standard legal disclaimer that what has worked for me may not work for you.

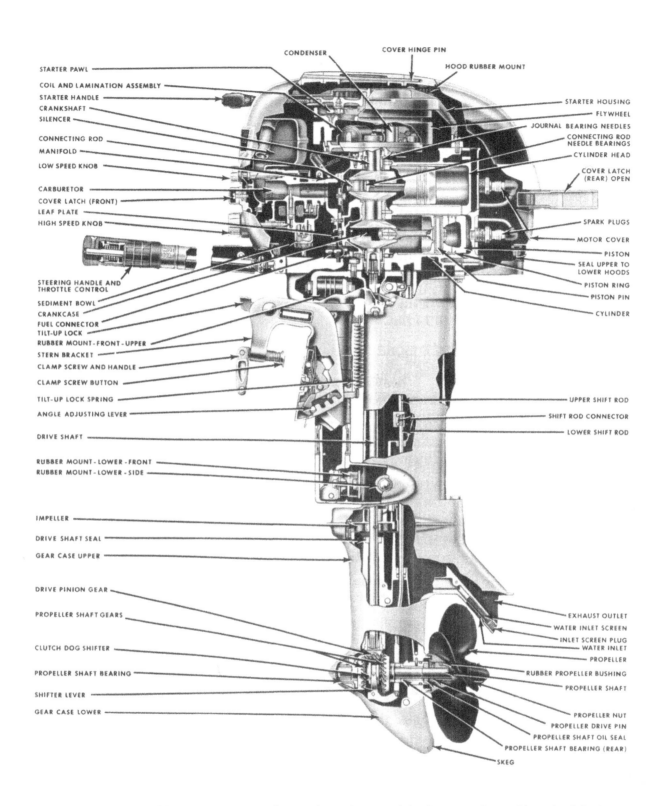

STARTER PAWL
COIL AND LAMINATION ASSEMBLY
STARTER HANDLE
CRANKSHAFT
SILENCER
CONNECTING ROD
MANIFOLD
LOW SPEED KNOB
CARBURETOR
COVER LATCH (FRONT)
LEAF PLATE
HIGH SPEED KNOB
STEERING HANDLE AND THROTTLE CONTROL
SEDIMENT BOWL
CRANKCASE
FUEL CONNECTOR
TILT-UP LOCK
RUBBER MOUNT-FRONT-UPPER
STERN BRACKET
CLAMP SCREW AND HANDLE
CLAMP SCREW BUTTON
TILT-UP LOCK SPRING
ANGLE ADJUSTING LEVER
DRIVE SHAFT
RUBBER MOUNT-LOWER-FRONT
RUBBER MOUNT-LOWER-SIDE
IMPELLER
DRIVE SHAFT SEAL
GEAR CASE UPPER
DRIVE PINION GEAR
PROPELLER SHAFT GEARS
CLUTCH DOG SHIFTER
PROPELLER SHAFT BEARING
SHIFTER LEVER
GEAR CASE LOWER

CONDENSER
COVER HINGE PIN
HOOD RUBBER MOUNT
STARTER HOUSING
FLYWHEEL
JOURNAL BEARING NEEDLES
CONNECTING ROD NEEDLE BEARINGS
CYLINDER HEAD
COVER LATCH (REAR) OPEN
SPARK PLUGS
MOTOR COVER
PISTON
SEAL UPPER TO LOWER HOODS
PISTON RING
PISTON PIN
CYLINDER
UPPER SHIFT ROD
SHIFT ROD CONNECTOR
LOWER SHIFT ROD
EXHAUST OUTLET
WATER INLET SCREEN
INLET SCREEN PLUG
WATER INLET
PROPELLER
RUBBER PROPELLER BUSHING
PROPELLER SHAFT
PROPELLER NUT
PROPELLER DRIVE PIN
PROPELLER SHAFT OIL SEAL
PROPELLER SHAFT BEARING (REAR)
SKEG

Much more detail of the components of an outboard motor. It looks complicated but don't let it over-whelm you. Remember that we are interested in outboards that need minor repairs, not major over-hauls. If you are successful in that pursuit, you will never get the chance to become personally acquainted with many of the parts labeled here.

Your Introduction to Old Outboard Motors (and a few words about mine)

When I was in my early teens, way back in the early 1970s, I was given an aluminum john boat as a Christmas present. Later that spring I received for my birthday present, a pair of oars with which to row that john boat. Of course, having an outboard would have been the ideal propulsion solution, but as I had no more present-receiving opportunities before summer and boating season, I was going to have to find an outboard on my own. Eventually I was able to purchase, for $25.00, an old 7.8 HP Voyager outboard, a brand that was obsolete and obscure even in the early 1970s. Manufactured in 1957 by a company that shut down in 1958, there were few replacement parts available for the old Voyager. Although I could get the outboard to actually run, it refused to run correctly, usually stalling within a moment of starting. Ignoring my total lack of knowledge of outboard repair, I went to work on the Voyager. Afterwards, the thing refused to run at all. After

beating myself half to death trying the keep it running, the Voyager was relegated to the corner of the basement, where my little brother (who went on the earn a degree in engineering) totally disassembled it to see what the insides looked like. I spent the rest of the summer rowing that john boat.

The mistakes I made with the Voyager are the mistakes that I will try to prevent you from making. The first mistake was purchasing an "orphan" brand of outboard for which few replacement parts were available. The plan, of course, is to find an outboard that requires few new parts to begin with, and it is not necessary that *all* parts be available. Since our goal is to avoid engines that need overhauls, we really don't care if overhaul parts such as pistons and rings are available. What we want to be able to find, and to buy at a reasonable price, are ignition parts, carburetor rebuild kits, water pump impellers, and recoil starter springs, to name a few. These are the parts that are frequently replaced and I will suggest that you replace them on your engine, even if you think you can get by without replacing them. And it is preferable that these actually be "new" parts. Collectors of old outboards speak of N.O.S (New Old Stock) parts. These are replacement parts that have been sitting on someone's shelves for years. Even though that rubber water pump impeller may be "new" in-the-box, if it was actually manufactured 30 or 40 years ago, can you count on it to last very long in your engine? Another problem with N.O.S parts is that they are usually expensive if that is all that is available. So we want our replacement parts to be of relatively recent manufacture if not current production.

The second mistake I made with the Voyager was not learning all that I could about the engine prior to beginning the repairs. At that time there were no repair books such as this one, only a service manual that assumed I knew more than I did and which made for very dry reading. Again, that is the purpose of this book: to compliment the service manual by providing additional instruction and information on simple repairs; choose your old outboard well and simple repairs will be all it needs.

Figure 0.03
If you don't need to travel fast, a Johnson or Evinrude 3 HP, made from 1952 until 1968, is a very common engine that is very easy to work on if you can live without a neutral and you are content to travel at sub-planing speeds.

Now, I absolutely *hate* to work on cars and some may find it an anomaly that I like to work on old outboards, but there are reasons for that. Modern automobiles are marvels of complication in order to meet the emissions,

safety and performance standards of today. Old outboards, however, are just like the cars of the 1950s. When you open the hood on a 1957 Chevy you are not greeted by a "wall-to-wall" mass of hoses, wires and unidentifiable objects. Instead, you see just an engine with vast open space surrounding it that invites you to climb into the compartment and sit on the fender where you can not only see all of the spark plugs, but actually reach all of them. No special wrench required. An old outboard is equally simple, and when mounted on a stand or even a saw horse, is at a convenient height for one to work on while sitting. I have yet to have to crawl under an old outboard on a wheeled creeper.

People who build boats (another hobby of mine) like to talk about the "moaning chair"; a comfortable chair that you sit back in right after you realize that you've just "royally screwed up" something. The point being that once you realize you have a problem, stop the work and carefully consider your options. It may pay to walk away from the engine for a day or so to consider alternatives. Almost always a little time and thought will supply a reasonable solution to what you had immediately thought was an insurmountable problem. So don't get frustrated and beat the old outboard with a sledge hammer or do something else that may make matters worse. Give yourself a little time to consider the problem and have a little self confidence. Chances are you have successfully tackled projects of one sort or another that were much more complex than dealing with the fifty-year-old technology of an old outboard motor.

Figure 0.04
A late-1950s Buccaneer 25 HP outboard provides plenty of power for a lightweight 14 foot aluminum runabout. Never heard of Buccaneer? Read Chapter 1.

In the simplest of terms, an outboard motor is little more that an engine which clamps to the stern of a boat that spins a propeller in the water in order to push the boat. The basic engine itself, termed the power head, is fitted with a carburetor which mixes fuel and air in the proper ratios before the mixture is burned in the cylinders. The fuel consists of gasoline with special oil mixed in. Without exception, the outboards discussed in this book are 2-cycle or "2-stroke" engines, which means that they *must* have oil mixed in with the gasoline.

The ignition system, which supplies the "spark" to ignite the fuel/air mixture in the cylinders at the proper time, is a "magneto" system in all of the old outboards that are the subject of this book. This means that no battery is needed in order for these engines to run. The running engine generates the electric current needed for the spark.

In order to start the engine, a "recoil" or "rewind" starter is fitted. This is the same type of manual starter fitted to most gasoline-powered lawn mowers. You pull on the starter rope to start the engine, and the rope automatically rewinds itself. The recoil starter is frequently damaged due to improper starting technique; the starter handle should not be abruptly yanked, but rather it should be slowly pulled until the starter mechanism is felt to engage and then pulled briskly to start the engine.

The function of the lower unit is to transform the power from the power head into thrust in the water. This is accomplished by a right-angle gear set in the lower unit which couples the spinning vertical drive shaft from the power head to the horizontal propeller shaft and propeller. If the engine has a full forward-

Figure 0.05
Manufactured in the late 1940's, this 11-foot aluminum boat pre-dates Coast Guard and industry horsepower regulations, which would probably label it "overpowered" with a 1953 Evinrude 15 HP outboard motor. By the way, that '53 15 HP weighs less than most late-model 15's. Old outboards are not necessarily heavier than modern outboards. It is noisier, however; and it uses more gasoline.

neutral-reverse gearshift, then this "transmission" will be located in the lower unit. Also located in the lower unit is a pump which circulates water throughout the power head and exhaust passages for cooling. This cooling water is drawn from the water that the boat is floating in and is returned to lake/river/ocean

Figure 0.06
A 1958 Johnson 18 HP mounted on a 1957 polished aluminum Crestliner boat makes a classy rig to tool-around the lake in, at less cost than a used personal water craft. The Johnson (and Evinrude) 18's are easier to work on than the Mercury 20's, such as the 1969 Mercury 20 on the other boat, at least in my opinion.

after circulating through the outboard.

The bulk of the rest of the outboard motor allows the major components listed above to all work together. The exhaust housing or tower housing is the structure that the power head mounts on top of and the lower unit mounts on the bottom of. The exhaust housing also directs the exhaust gases from the power head to the exhaust outlets under water. The clamp brackets are used to clamp the outboard to the stern of a boat and often there will be rubber cushioned mounts incorporated into the clamp brackets/exhaust housing in order to lessen noise and vibration. The clamp bracket also has an adjustment feature which allows the opera-

tor to adjust the vertical angle of the outboard in order to obtain the most efficient operation of the outboard. The swivel function that provides steering is also incorporated into the clamp bracket/exhaust housing assemblies. The shroud (also called a hood or cowl) protects the power head from the weather.

Some outboard motors are fitted with tiller controls, meaning that the outboard is steering with a tiller or steering handle and that the operator must be seated next to the outboard in order to control it. Other outboards are fitted for remote controls, where the operator can be seated some distance away from the outboard and the boat is steered with a steering wheel while shift and throttle control is by remote-mounted levers. Chapters 13, 14, and 15 discuss converting outboards to these different modes of control.

The primary concern of everyone on the water should be safety. All to often the evening news includes details of someone injured or

Figure 0.07
Small boat designer Jim Michalak, author of *Boatbuilding for Beginners (and Beyond)*, cruising a midwestern lake in his 18 foot cabin skiff which he built to his own design and powered with an early 1960's Gale 15 HP outboard purchased at a swap meet for $100.

killed in a boating accident. A safety feature found on virtually all new outboard motors, but almost never seen on old ones, is a safety "kill" switch which shuts off the outboard should the operator be thrown from the boat. Chapter 11 will detail how one of these switches can be installed on an older outboard. I recommend that you seriously consider adding one to your engine.

Figure 0.08
Jim Michalak's Gale 15 as it sat "for sale" at a swap meet. Manufactured by Outboard Marine Corp. (OMC), the same company that made Johnsons and Evinrudes, this "never-heard-of-it-before" outboard shares many of the same parts as the more well known engines, while typically costing less to buy. This engine required little in the way of repairs.

1

What to Buy

New outboard motors are expensive. After you pick yourself up off the floor after hearing that revelation, I would like to point out that, relatively speaking, they are no more expensive than they ever were. My father bought a brand-new 7.5 HP Mercury in 1975 for $420.00. A comparable outboard today would cost about four times that much, just as the brand-new 1978 Ford F150 4-wheel-drive pickup that I almost bought for $5,900.00 would, today, cost about four times as much.

Still, for many the cost of a new outboard motor places it way towards the bottom of the "priority" list, behind such essential items as rent, utility bills, and groceries. So the potential power boater starts perusing the racks of used outboards at the local boat dealerships where it is quickly discovered that a good, used, late-model outboard motor costs but a little less than the new ones. The classified advertisements in the Sunday newspaper show that private owners of late-model outboards seem to be aware of the value of their engines, and the few engines that show some promise are usually already "sold," often it seems before the newspaper has hit the street. Obviously, looking for used, late-model outboards is not going to save you much money.

Although outboard motors have been around since the turn of the 20th century, it was in the 1950s that the popularity of outboards and outboard boats really boomed. It was in the early 1950s that the full forward-neutral-reverse gearshift and the remote fuel tank became widely available on outboard motors and those features, along with the relative prosperity of a growing middle class, really fueled a boom in boating, particularly outboard boating. In 1956 alone, about 750,000 outboard motors were sold, more than in any one year before or since. Even if the total num-

Figure 01-01
They had it right back in the '50s; a day of fishing was supposed to be a day of relaxation, not competition. V6 outboards, metal flake bass boats, and assorted electronics may increase the catch, but do they really increase the enjoyment?

ber of stern drive boats is added, today's outboard unit sales still fall short of the boom years of the 1950s. In 1956 the largest outboards widely available were only 40 HP, and the largest units available from Outboard Marine Corporation (OMC), the largest manufacturer of outboard motors, were only 30 HP.

A curious fact for which I have no real explanation is that few people will throw out an old outboard motor. While it is difficult to find very old lawnmowers and very old vacuum cleaners (not that anyone would want to) hidden in the dark corners of basements and garages, it is quite common to find very old outboard motors residing in such places. Perhaps it is the happy memories of fishing with grandpa or water-skiing with the cousins which makes old outboards seem worth keeping (as opposed to the work associated with running a lawn mower or a vacuum cleaner) but the fact remains that few people will "toss" an old outboard.

It is a sad fact of life that many (most) of us don't have as much leisure time as we would like, and the people of the 1950s and 1960s were no different. Few of the thousands of outboards sold were ever run enough to be worn out. Just guessing, I would say that less than 5 percent of the old outboards I have had

Figure 01-03
A nicely repainted 1956 10 HP Johnson has been given a new set of reproduction decals. You may not care what your outboard looks like as long as it runs reliably, but if you do care, you can certainly repaint it in original (or close to original) colors, and reproduction decals are available for the more common models. Many outboard collectors repaint outboards with aerosol automotive touch-up paint which is available in so many colors that almost always you can find a color which closely approximates the original outboard paint. No need for a compressor or spray gun, nor the skill to use them.

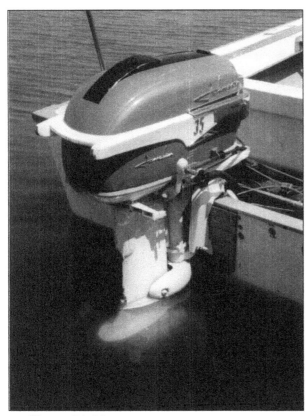

Figure 01-02
A 1957 35 HP Johnson. There are a lot of these late 1950s 2-cylinder outboards around in both the standard "Holiday Bronze" paint or in the upscale Javelin trim version shown here. Equally prevalent in Evinrude versions, these "Big Twin" engines are often cheaper to buy than smaller engines. They came in both tiller-control and remote control versions, and are easy to convert back and forth.

over the last ten years could be considered worn-out from use, although a somewhat greater number were in need of overhauls due to abuse rather than use. Abuse and poor repairs are bigger killers of old outboards than overuse.

So plenty of old outboard motors were sold and plenty of them still exist, often hidden away and forgotten. To be truthful, some of these engines are in such poor condition as to be junk, but many were lightly used and prop-

erly stored and require only minor repairs to be placed back into running condition. In my opinion these old (maybe very old) outboards can represent good value for the person looking for the most "push" from his limited boating budget, provided that he is willing to learn how to work on the engine himself. At labor rates of $70.00 an hour or more, most big-name outboard dealerships refuse to work on outboard motors over thirty years old, fearing that the invoice will exceed the value of the engine and the owner will never come back to retrieve his repaired engine and settle up. This is often the reason for an older outboard languishing in the basement corner; it needs some

Figure 01-04
While not in "show-room-new" condition, this 7½ HP Johnson is still a good looking engine as-is. A little work and it could be a reliable source of power for your boat.

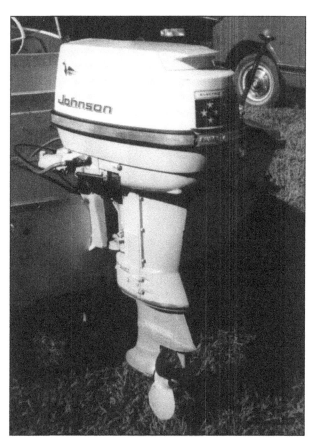

Figure 01-05
A 40 HP Johnson from the mid-60s; a good engine as long as one avoids the 1960 and 1961 models, as well as the electric shift versions (see text).

minor repair but the shop won't touch it and the owner doesn't want to mess with it. This is opportunity knocking on your door.

I recommend that an individual looking for inexpensive outboard power, and who has no real interest in outboards other than in pushing his boat, should buy an OMC (Outboard Marine Corp.)-built product made from 1955

Figure 01-06
This 1953 25 HP Evinrude is a bit older than I would recommend. In my opinion the oldest engines you should be looking at are 1955s. By that time the designs were pretty much standardized and finalized and there were very few big changes until almost 1970. Note that this engine is a manual-start version with tiller control. It can be converted to electric start if you can find the parts, but if you really want electric start I would suggest looking for an engine that already has it. Adapting this engine to remote control is a piece of cake.

to 1974. Usually (but not always) carrying the Johnson or Evinrude brand names, these OMC-built engines are as easy to work on, and as easy to learn how to work on, as an outboard can be. And you will need to work on it yourself. Even if you could find a shop willing to work on an outboard this old, the cost would be prohibitive. There is a breed of engine repair shop that will claim to work on "the outboards no one else wants to," and although I am sure there are a few reputable individuals out there, most of the ones that I am personally familiar with I would not deal with.

With very few exceptions, these old OMC engines have two cylinders, and they all will be 2-cycle or "2-stroke" engines. Their lubricating oil must be mixed with the gasoline. Unlike 4-cycle engines, such as in your automobile and most lawn mowers, 2-cycle engines do not have a crankcase into which you pour oil every now and then. Special oil must be mixed with the gasoline at the proper ratio for every tank of gasoline that you run through the engine; just a few minutes of running one of these 2-cycle outboards on oil-free gasoline will destroy it. I use the cheapest 2-cycle oil that I can find in the discount stores (other than the *really* cheap oil found in a few dollar stores, which has its contents labeled as "partially unknown") and I always mix in at least as much oil as the manufacturer originally recommended.

Most of these outboards were marked with their oil mix ratios but lacking that you usually can not go wrong with a 1950s or 1960s OMC by mixing at a ratio of 24 to 1, or by adding twice as much oil to the gasoline as for a 50 to 1 ratio, which is the ratio most modern outboards run. You might get away with running less oil than that, but in my opinion you are skating on thin ice. In fact it is my habit to run more oil than originally recommended. Just as the owner's manual of your car tells you to change the oil more frequently if your auto sees "severe service," I use more oil in my gasoline because my outboards occasionally see severe service. Back in the old days, running a fuel mixture heavy with oil could lead to spark plug fouling, where the electrode on the end of the spark plug becomes clogged with crud, causing the spark plug to stop sparking and the engine to stop running! But it has been over a decade since I have fouled a plug in an outboard motor. The new 2-cycle oils (even the cheap ones) are much better than the oils of fifty years ago, and fouled plugs are just not the concern they once were.

The other danger was piston ring fouling, where the rings became stuck in their piston grooves because of carbon build-up. Again that is an infrequent problem now, and there are carbon remover liquids that you can buy and mix with the gasoline to eliminate that concern. I occasionally mix a bit of carbon removing in my gasoline, usually only once or twice a boating season.

I would not recommend that anyone other than a collector purchase a 1950s or even a 1960s Mercury. During this time period, Mercury was run by a man best characterized as "strange." This was reflected in the engines by lots of weird stuff like fine threads, left-hand threads, and assemblies requiring lots of special tools for disassembly (Figure 01-07).

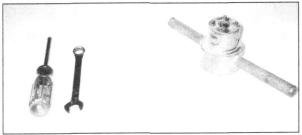

Figure 01-07
The tools on the left are the types of tools needed to replace the water pump impeller in a 1950's or 1960's OMC outboard; the tool on the right is the special tool needed to change the water pump impeller in just one 1950s Mercury model (other models require other special tools). Which of these tools do you already own? Which of these tools would be easier to find and cheaper to buy if you needed them?

Many Mercurys suffer from weak lower units. The late 50s Mercury Mark 25s (18 to 20 HP) are often found with bad lower units. Later 1960s and early 1970s 20 HP Mercurys have the same weakness (Figure 01-08).

Figure 01-08
A rack of Mercurys, mostly 20 HP models (that's a 9.8 on the left). Note how many of these are missing their lower units. Weak lower units are a common problem with the smaller models. The "swept back" housings were thin and easily broken, while the design of the shifting mechanism resulted in a propeller shaft that was hollow and had a large slot milled (cut) into it.

Other weird things about old Mercurys include little lead seals on the crankcases so that dealers could tell if an owner had disassembled the engine, thereby voiding the warranty. (If the engine was still covered by the warranty, why would the owner be trying to fix it himself?) Late 50s and early 60s Mercurys from 10 to 25 HP featured an "automatic transmission" that made water pump impeller replacement an almost impossible task—steer well clear of Mercurys of that era that feature both the shift and the throttle combined in the twist grip. (Figure 01-09)

Figure 01-09
Any late-1950s or early-60s Mercury that has the shift and throttle combined into the tiller twist grip is an "automatic transmission" model. Changing a water pump impeller on one of these is a major undertaking. You would have a hard time finding a Mercury dealership with someone who knows how to work on these models, which is okay as they probably would not have the necessary special tools anyway.

Collectors love old Mercs, but I would not recommend them to someone just looking for a cheap outboard motor.

The outboard motor business in the 1950s was like the computer business in the 1980s and early 1990s—everybody and their brother was selling outboards. You could buy, in addi-

Figure 01-10
While I always recommend that the novice avoid all old Mercurys, this one is something to RUN away from as fast as you can. An early 1960s Mercury 6-cylinder 70 HP is not the project for a novice, nor is any 6-cylinder Mercury.

tion to the names everyone has heard of, West Bend outboards (yes, the cookware company), Martin outboards (Presto pressure cookers), Champions, Scott-Atwater's (Figure 01-11), Voyagers, Majestics, Sea Kings, Sea Flyers, Sea Bees, Gales, Hiawathas, Sabers, Elgins (Figure 01-12), etc. etc. Although some of these long-forgotten outboards are of interest to collectors, I would recommend that someone just looking for a cheap outboard avoid most of them. New replacement parts are often hard to

Figure 01-11
A really nice 5 HP Scott with a full forward-neutral-reverse gearshift. Don't be tempted. Leave it for the collectors of old outboard motors.

Figure 01-12
A row of Elgin outboards for sale at a swap meet. Sold by Sears and manufactured by West Bend (yep, the cookware people). I would avoid these even though they are often cheap to buy. Parts are difficult to come by and expensive when they can be had.

come by, expensive, and usually are NOS (New-old stock). "Parts engines" are the usual source of parts for this type of engine, and you may need to have three or four parts engines laying around to have the parts you need.

There is an exception to the "off-brand" recommendation, however. Everyone has heard of Evinrude and Johnson, the two OMC brand names, but until 1963, there was a third division of OMC selling outboards, the Gale division. Gales were the "cheap" engines, and were often sold by sporting goods and hardware stores, whereas the "flagship" Johnson and Evinrude brands were sold only through

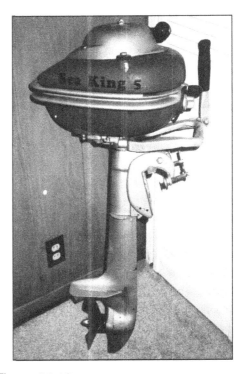

Figure 01-13
A late 1940s 5 HP Montgomery Ward's "Sea King" built by the Gale division of OMC (also the makers of Johnson and Evinrude) this engine was produced at a time when the management of OMC felt it was best for their various divisions to actually compete with each other, and so the engines of each division were unique to that division.

boat dealerships. Gale also wholesaled engines to department stores and other retailers, which would put their own name on them. The most common Gales are Montgomery Ward Sea Kings (Figure 01-13). Goodyear Tires stores sold Sea Bees and Fedway stores sold Sabers: most of these were made by OMC, and in some, but not all, cases are almost carbon-copies of Evinrudes and Johnsons (Figure 01-14).

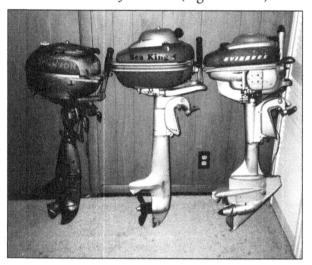

Figure 01-14
"Sisters" but not "triplets": The engine on the left is a 1949 Johnson 5 HP; the engine in the center is a 1949 Gale 5 HP; the engine on the right is a1949 Evinrude 5.4 HP. The three engines pictured have virtually no common parts, despite all being built by OMC. By 1955, Evinrude and Johnson engines were identical except for cosmetic details, and the Gale models were moving steadily in that same direction.

For example, if you run across a 1950s 5HP outboard with full forward-neutral-reverse gearshift, and wearing the "Brooklure" name (sold by the Spiegel catalog people made famous on "Lets Make a Deal"; Figure 01-15), you have found an engine very similar to the "Johnyrude" (outboard collector's term) 5½ HP. The same ignition parts, water pump impeller,

Figure 01-15
Gale wholesaled outboards to several department store chains and also to Speigel, who labeled the engines "Brooklures" and sold them though their catalog. This 5 HP Brooklure is in good cosmetic condition, and while not identical to its 5½ Johnson and Evinrude contemporaries, it is close enough that most of the commonly replaced parts are the same.

and carburetor rebuild kits will fit, but don't expect the kid at the Johnson or Evinrude dealership's parts counter to know this, or his parts books to reflect this. If that 5 HP Brooklure only has a neutral clutch, however, and no reverse other that rotating the engine around 180 degrees, then you have a completely different engine (Figure 01-16); the

Figure 01-16
This 5 HP Gale has no gearshift and is unlike any Johnson or Evinrude model. It even has little in common with the Gale-built engine in Figure 01-15. Very few new parts are available for these unique Gale engines and I would advise avoiding them even through they are common and cheap. Look for Gales with the full Forward-Neutral-Reverse gearshift and 1955 or newer.

versions.

When dealing with Johnsons and Evinrudes of up to about 1959 (1960 in the case of the 5½) be aware that the models that used remote gas tanks did not come equipped with fuel pumps (see Chapter 8). These engines used a "dual passage hose" similar to welding torch dual hose, and actually pressurized the fuel tank through one side of the hose, which forced gasoline up the other side of the hose to the motor. If you open the cowling of one of these engines and see two hoses attached to the motor-side quick connector fitting, then that motor uses a pressure tank and be sure that you get a good tank and quick connect fitting with the tank (Figure 01-17).

These special tanks are no longer made, and refurbishing and selling old pressure tanks is a

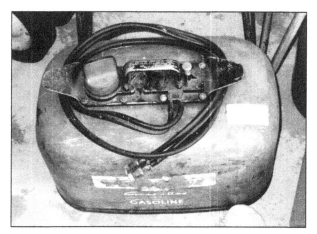

Figure 01-17
A "pressure" fuel tank, as used on Johnsons and Evinrudes in the 1950s. Note the double hose and special connector. These tanks are no longer available new and command a high price on online auction sites. They are somewhat cheaper at antique outboard motor swap meets. Chapter 8 covers problems and repairs of pressure tanks, while Chapter 12 provides details for converting a pressure tank motor to use a fuel pump.

ignition parts will still work, but not the carb kits or pump impeller. The power heads are completely different. If the 5 HP Brooklure has no neutral at all, then there is no inter-changeability of parts with the "Johnyrudes". The versions of these Gale engines that have many common parts with the flagship models can be good values, because the engines are usually cheaper to buy than the "name-brand" profitable side line for some of the little motor repair shops that will work on these engines. Yes, most of these engines can be converted to use fuel pumps and standard outboard fuel tanks, but it is an added expense (see Chapter 12). The 5½ HP is the hardest to convert. One odd note is that the cheaper Gale-versions of OMC engines came factory-fitted with fuel pumps a couple of years before the flagship brands had them. Go figure.

All OMC engines up to 40 HP made from about 1952 until the late 1960s had one common weak point: the magneto coils. These engines have two coils (one for each cylinder), and if the original coils have not been replaced, they will need to be replaced. A dealership will charge about twenty-five bucks per coil plus an hour of labor to replace them. Through the Antique Outboard Motor Club (www.aomci.org), you can find sources where you can buy these coils for fourteen or fifteen bucks, and installing them yourself will give you the opportunity to also replace the ignition points and condensers (about fifteen bucks) and the sparkplug wires (copper core only—don't use graphite wires.) This will give your engine a virtually new ignition system at a fraction of the cost of a single "black box" for an electronic ignition system.

This is why I avoid electronic ignition. Marketing experts have spent lots of money convincing the public that electronic ignition is better that "old-fashioned" points and condensers. Compare the prices of replacement parts for both systems and then decide.

Various models of OMC outboards have specific weaknesses, but often not every version or model-year is affected. Let's look at OMC engines of about 10 HP. The 10 HP Johnson (Evinrude version came out a few years later) with full gear shift was introduced in 1949 and was made until about 1964. From 1965 until 1974, a "low-profile" 9½ was made. I would avoid the 1949 to 1954 versions, as there was much experimenting going on and not much uniformity from year to year. The powerhead design was pretty much standardized from 1955 to 1964, the main changes being an improved recoil starter for 1956 and a fuel pump added in 1960. The lower unit used from 1955 to 1957 was a good solid unit that also saw service on 12, 15, and 18 HP engines, so it is plenty strong for the 10. However, in 1958 OMC switched the 10 to a smaller lower unit, and it is very common to see 1958 through 1964 10 HP engines with lower unit problems or missing lower units. The later 9½s are fairly common, but in making this engine "low profile" so fishermen could fish over it, OMC crammed all the stuff down into the housing and these engines are a pain in the butt to work on. So, when it comes to 10 HP (+/-) OMC engines, I usually only have an interest in 1955s through 1957s, and I prefer 1956 and 1957 due to the stronger recoil starter unit. Of course, at the right price I would buy any of the above engines if it were in good condition. Collectors love the very early 10s.

The usual failure mode for an OMC 5½ HP is for it to toss the lower connecting rod through the crankcase. So a 5½ with a bad power head but good lower unit is not worth much, because the power head is the hard part to find. Conversely, a 1962 10 HP with a bad power head and a good lower unit can be a good buy, because there are plenty of 10s of that vintage around with lower unit problems.

If you are looking for "big iron," say a 40 HP, there are some models which I would suggest you avoid. The first one to avoid is any 40 HP with electric shift; if the engine does not have a shift lever on the starboard (that is, on the right, looking forward) side of the engine, it is an electric shift version, and these have a very poor reputation. The shifting of the lower unit was handled by electromagnets instead of mechanically, and having electrical components in the lower unit where they can get wet was a bad idea. The other 40s to avoid would be the 1960 and 1961 models; the 40s built during these first two years of production had a reputation for breaking crankshafts. The basic problem is that the 40 was a "bored-out" 35 HP, while the 35 HP was a "bored-out" 30 HP, which was a "bored-out" 25 HP. The factory just kept increasing the bore size of the cylinders without making any major changes to the engine block and crankshaft, and those components where just plain over-stressed at 40 HP. For the 1962 model year, OMC gave the 40 HP a completely redesigned power head with a new block, new crankshaft, new pistons, new connecting rods, and a new flywheel. The 1962's and later 40s (except for the electric shift versions) are very robust, reliable engines. The 1960s and 1961's are not (Figure 01-18).

In this book I will refer to these larger (25 HP to 40 HP) engines as "Big Twins," a term that Evinrude used but as the Johnson versions

Figure 01-18
Time for a pop quiz: Which of the above motors (A, B, or C) do I recommend you avoid buying?
Answer, "All of the above."
A is an "automatic transmission" Mercury
B is a very early 1950s version of the Johnson 10 HP
C is a 1960 Evinrude 40 HP

were more or less identical except for cosmetics I use the term for all of these engines. I will also use the generic term "OMC" (Outboard Marine Corp.) when it does not make a difference whether the subject engine is an Evinrude, a Johnson, or a Gale (Figure 01-19).

Now comes the part that everyone has been waiting for: how much are these things worth? I am aware of only one price guide in existence for outboards dating back into the 1960s and earlier, and it will be discussed in Chapter 3. But basically, an old outboard motor is worth what a seller is willing to sell it for and a buyer is willing to pay. It is as simple as that. The novice outboard buyer can protect himself by setting limits as to how much money he intends to spend on an old outboard and not exceeding that without good reason. Unless

01-19

A 25 HP Gale version of the Big Twin. The Big Twins are sort of like "big block" engines and are OMC outboards of from 25 HP to 40 HP, from 1950 until about the mid 1970s (except for some very late 1960s/early 1970s 25s, which were based on the "small block" 18 HP engine).

the owner can demonstrate the engine on a boat (not in a bucket of water; an engine may run in a drum of water but may not run "right" on a boat) always assume the outboard will need repairs and replacement parts and that you will have to put time and money into it. The novice can also protect himself by deciding in advance which series or horsepower engine he is interested in buying, and only buying engines in that horsepower range or series, so that any duds purchased can become parts engines for a better example.

In my area (Midwest) and at the time of this writing, I believe that a 1950s to early 1960s OMC outboard in fairly decent mechanical condition, but maybe not real pretty, can be

bought for no more than $150.00 and often for no more than $100.00. I suggest this is a rough price range for you to stay in, with the understanding that the situation may be different in your particular area and that showroom-new examples can sell for much more. A more general guideline is that a used old OMC can be bought for about 20 percent of the cost of a new outboard of similar horsepower, and often for less. Old outboards in showroom-new condition can cost 30 to 40 percent of the cost of a new outboard.

An anomaly of the old outboard market is that prices do not vary much in relation to horsepower, i.e., a 1956 3 HP will often sell for about the same as a 1956 30 HP in similar condition. But while there is potential to save more money in the larger engines, the purchase of a small used outboard can still save you significant money compared to buying a new one.

You probably already have some idea what horsepower range you are looking for, especially if you already have a boat. An aspect that you may not have given much thought to, however, is what "shaft length" you need. First, a bit of background info on shaft lengths. It evolved in the early days of outboard motors that they would be, generally, designed for mounting on a boat transom measuring 15 inches in height. Later, when it became apparent that increased freeboard might be desirable on larger boats, a second "standard" of a 20-inch-high transom was established. The 15-inch engines were referred to as "standard" or "short" shaft engines, while the 20-inch engines were referred to as "long" shaft engines. Through most of the 1950s and 1960s, nearly all outboards (there were exceptions) were available in either version, although as the engines become larger and larger—exceeding 100 HP in the early 1960s, and exceeding 150 HP in the mid 1970s—most of the bigger engines were only available in the 20-inch "long" shaft version. In the late 1980s, with the increased popularity of deep-V offshore boats, outboards designed for 25-inch transoms began to be available, although these are almost always engines in excess of 100 HP. Only the smallest of engines, say under 40 HP, are still available in the 15-inch "short" shaft version. Because of confusion caused by the introduction of the 25-inch engines, which are sometimes referred to as "long" shaft engines, leaving the 20-inchers to be called "short" shafts, I suggest we dispense with all the "short" and "long" nomenclature, and instead refer to the particular engines by the inch measurements, and since we are discussing old engines, that will limit us to 15-inch and 20-inch engines.

First of all, how do we distinguish a 15-inch engine from a 20-inch engine? This is fairly easy with OMC (Johnson, Evinrude, and Gale) engines, as the 20-inch versions from the 1950s and 60s, of no more than 40 HP, always had an adapter piece added to the "leg" of the engine. Shown are photos of two 1957 Johnson 18 HP outboard motors, identical except that one is a 15-inch engine, and the other is a 20-inch engine (Figure 01-20). It is fairly easy to pick out the adapter section added just above the lower unit of the 20-inch engine. If you carry a tape measure or yard

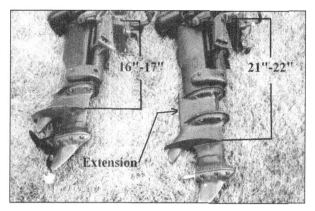

01-20
The left engine is a "short shaft" (15-inch) while the engine on the right is a "long shaft" (20-inch). Note the extension on the "long shaft" engine.

stick, you can always measure the distance from the underside of the outboard's mounting clamps (the point which actually sits on top of the transom) to the horizontal cavitation plate located just above the propeller. This dimension will be about 16 or 17 inches on a "15-inch" motor, and will be about 21 or 22 inches on a "20-inch motor."

The sharp-minded reader will ask, "can a 15-inch engine be converted to a 20-inch version, and also the other-way-around?" The short answer is "Yes." But there are several parts necessary to make the conversion, and these parts may be difficult to find. So it is probably best to try to buy the version of the engine that you need, rather than count on a conversion. Now, how do you identify which engine a particular boat is set up to use? Again the yardstick or ruler will come in handy; you merely measure the height of the transom at the motor mounting point (Figure 01-21). If that measurement is 15 to 16 inches, then the transom is for a 15-inch outboard. A measurement of 20 to 21 inches indicates that a 20-

01-21
How to measure the transom height on your boat. Note that the measurement is made with the T-square (or yard stick or whatever) held vertically, and not along the face of the transom.

inch engine is called for. Just one complication; the "height" of the transom is the vertical measurement from the engine mounting point down to the plane of the boat's bottom. Since the transom will have some "rake" to it, the yard stick will only touch the top of the transom, not the bottom. The measurement is *not* made by holding the yardstick directly on the transom. Note that few transoms will measure at exactly 15 or 20 inches, and that most motors have about an extra inch or so of length. It generally will not cause any harm to have the lower unit a little deeper in the water than what would be ideal, but an engine mounted too shallow may have problems with cooling water circulation and propeller ventilation (air getting into the prop, causing it to lose its "bite" on the water and causing the engine to rev up as the boat slows down).

I have already mentioned that most models of outboards were originally available in either the 15-inch or the 20-inch version. But that does not mean that there are equal numbers of each version out there waiting to be found. For example, if you intend to power your boat with a used OMC-built outboard of under 20 HP, and older than 1970, you will find many more 15-inch versions than 20-inch versions, simply because most boats of that era in that horsepower-range came with 15-inch transoms. I would guess that about 98 percent of such engines that I have seen are 15-inchers. If, however you intend to use a 40 HP OMC outboard dating from, say 1962 until 1982, then you will probably find used engines split about 50/50 between 15-inch and 20-inch versions. Larger engines, say 60 HP and above, 1962 and newer, will almost always be 20-inch versions, probably about 95 percent. These percentages are my guesses based on looking at an awful lot of outboards, and not based on any hard research. Also, local characteristics may affect those percentages. Geographic areas containing large numbers of sailboats, for example, will offer more 20-inch versions of smaller outboards than geographic areas with few sailboats. A perusal of local boat dealers' used motor displays will give you a clue as to what is common in your particular area. One final comment: Don't rely on asking the owner what the shaft length is on his old outboard; about half the time the answer you get will be wrong. You need to be able the determine this yourself.

2

Where to Find It

Before you even consider buying or bartering for an old outboard motor, you need to do a little research as to the legalities of outboard motor ownership in your particular state. Some states require outboard motors to be titled just as autos are titled. For example, I live in Missouri, not far from the Mississippi River which forms the state line with Illinois. Missouri titles outboard motors, and Illinois does not. If my neighbor down the street is cleaning out his garage and unearths an old outboard motor he had long forgotten he had, he might offer it to me for a pittance. I would point out the white registration decal of the state of Missouri on it and ask him about the title. His reply will most likely be that he has no idea what he did with the title and just wants to get the greasy thing out of his garage so his wife will quit "bugging" him about the messy garage and am I interested in it or not? The asking price is less than the cost of a propeller for a new outboard.

If I want to legally use this outboard in the State of Missouri, I am going to have to convince my neighbor that it is worth his while to apply for a duplicate title so he can sign it over to me. That is about the only way I am going to get legal title to this old outboard. Now let's

complicate matters a bit; let's say that my neighbor, upon being shown the Missouri registration decal, scratches his head and says that he did not know that outboards had to be titled and that he bought this outboard about 10 years ago at a garage sale. Well, you can go to the Dept. of Motor Vehicles (the state agency that handles outboard motor registration in Missouri; other states may use other agencies) and get the name and last-known address of whoever is named on the title, and then try to hunt them up to see if they will "sign over" title to the motor. Just how bad do you want this outboard motor? But it can get worse. Let's say the neighbor says he bought this outboard about ten years ago at an estate sale; so the last registered owner of this motor is no longer with us.

And just about the time my neighbor is starting to tire of my questions concerning paperwork that he does not have, a guy driving a car with Illinois license plates pulls up and asks if that greasy, old outboard motor laying by the curb is for sale. My neighbor says sure it's for sale, and cheap too, but he does not have a title to it. The man from Illinois says that is not a problem as Illinois does not title outboard motors. Five minutes later the man from Illinois drives off with a greasy outboard motor in his trunk and my neighbor goes back to work cleaning his garage with a bit of cash in his pocket.

But let's back up a moment. What if this outboard did not have the registration decal? What if there was no evidence of it being titled in Missouri or in any other state? If the motor had not been titled in Missouri, and showed no evidence of being stolen or titled in another state, then I *could* get a Missouri title to it. All I would have to do is obtain the necessary forms (three or four of them) from the Department of Motor Vehicles, take the motor and the forms to a Missouri State Water Patrol Officer (who will check to see if the motor has been reported stolen or if it shows signs of having been titled in another state), and then take the completed forms back to the Department of Motor Vehicles, where I can pay the customary fees and be issued a title. Yes, it is a royal pain. And can be an even bigger pain if, despite the lack of a registration decal, it turns out the motor was in fact already titled. Maybe the previous owner forgot to apply the decal, or maybe it fell off. Or better yet, what if the outboard turns out to be stolen?

If you have no clue where to find out about outboard motor titling and registration requirements in your area, check with a local boat dealer who can certainly direct you to the correct state agency. But don't believe everything the boat dealer tells you; I have had them give me incorrect information before. Being familiar with your local outboard motor licensing/titling regulations is a necessary prerequisite to buying old outboard motors.

There is a new legal issue on the horizon (closer than the horizon for people in some areas, such as California): bans on the use of 2-cycle engines on some specific lakes and in some specific areas, Lake Tahoe being the best known. It is an undebatable fact that older outboard motors are just not "environmentally friendly." They dump a considerable portion of the fuel they use into the water, and seeping

lower units can add some gear oil as well. Certainly there are those among the readers whose conscience will not allow them to run any outboard other than the most modern fuel-efficient, environmentally-friendly engines, and I commend you for putting your principles above the need for economy. But I will not condemn those who must, because of financial considerations, either minimize their expenditure on their outboard motor or do without one.

My personal position is that I try to compensate in other areas of my life for whatever environmental damage my all-too-infrequent opportunities to go boating inflict on the waters. I only drive small pickup trucks (and I have ever since sitting in the "gas lines" of 1979 in a V8-powered SUV back when no one knew what an SUV was) and I take advantage of opportunities to go boating in my home-built sail-, paddle-, and oar-powered boats when an appropriate situation presents itself. I also take some pride in using an existing asset that otherwise might end up in a landfill. Whatever your personal position on old outboards, however, keep in mind that leaving an oil sheen on the water is a direct violation of Federal and some state laws that you can be held accountable for. So it would be in your best interest to replace hoses and fittings and gaskets as necessary to minimize any leakage from your engine, for legal reasons if not for moral ones.

Once you have decided that an older outboard is the best option for you, then comes the problem of actually finding a suitable one. Usually, the first place people want to look for old outboards is in the Sunday classified section of the newspaper. Other than maybe perusing the "bargain box" section, I would skip the newspaper. If someone is spending the money to place a newspaper advertisement, they probably feel that their outboard has a lot of value, certainly more than you want to spend. And if it is indeed a bargain, chances are it is probably already sold anyway. Personally, back in the days when I was actively hunting old outboards, I spent little time checking the classified ads.

Figure 02-01
A dry meet sponsored by a local chapter of the Antique Outboard Motor Club, Inc. "Dry" means a meet at a location that is not on the water; in this case, the meet was held at a vocational-technical school with a marine repair curriculum. One will find items for sale and also items just being shown at these meets.

Local boat dealers can be a good source of old outboards, but don't bother looking at the used outboards on the showroom rack; they are ready to run but priced as such. No, what you want to look at is the pile of old outboards out back; the "scrap pile." Over the years I have purchased, or traded for, several decent old outboards out of the scrap pile of one par-

ticular local dealer, but it took a while for him to get to know me before he would even let me look at the pile. I earned his respect by never wasting his time haggling over money; I would point out the engine I was interested in and he would shoot me a price; I would either pay the price or "pass" on the engine. Another local outboard collector was "banned" from this dealership because he always wanted to dicker on the price. The cheap S.O.B. (Strange Outboard Boater) almost had all of us collectors banned from the property. Although the first couple of outboards I bought from the dealer were probably overpriced, as time went by and he got to know me his prices came down quite a bit. Still later I found I could purchase new galvanized boat trailers from this dealer at his cost by giving him my order months in advance and then waiting until he needed to have other trailers delivered from the trailer factory, about 200 miles away. I would take a vacation day from work and drive down to the trailer factory and bring back a "stack" of two or three trailers (one of which was mine). He would sell me mine at his cost in exchange for saving him the cost of sending an employee to retrieve the trailers. I bought three new boat trailers that way. The only downside to building a relationship with smaller boat dealers is that it takes time.

I mentioned the outboard motor collectors. I believe that a good place to start looking for old outboard motors is at a swap meet sponsored by the Antique Outboard Motor Club, Inc. This is a nationwide (international, actually) club with swap meets scheduled year-round. An online schedule of their swap meets can be found at their website, www.aomci.org and membership is usually not required to attend, nor is there usually an admission charge. Sometimes the hat will be passed to help pay for lunch if it is served.

Figure 02-02
A collector obviously looking to clean out his garage/basement/shop. You would be doing this guy a favor by buying one of his engines or some of his parts. As a collector I can assure you that he would *love* to go home with an empty pickup truck.

Collectors are usually attracted to engines that look "pretty". In other words, engines that are in excellent cosmetic condition, with showroom-condition paint and decals, and with all the original knobs. Engines in such condition are rare and they bring a premium price from a collector. But the price can drop significantly if the paint and decals are scratched and worn. If some of the knobs are missing and maybe if the cowling is dented, the price can drop even more. Yet bad paint and decals and missing knobs, in themselves, do not affect the running ability of an engine, although they may very well be signs of abuse

that should be investigated. If you can live with an "ugly" outboard (or if you are willing to put some time and money into new paint) you might find a bargain at a swap meet. Actually, considering the popularity of the "Antiques Road Show" television program, you might get a better deal from a collector at a swap meet than from the little old lady down the street who is convinced that anything "old" is worth big dollars. Most collectors end up with too many outboards and often will cull their collections in order to make room for more collectable examples, so there are often some real deals at the swap meets.

Figure 02-03
The outboard motors on the ground are for sale, but the restored early 1950s wooden boat is for show only. No way would these guys part with their pride and joy!

Another venue where I have had some success is the bulletin boards you often find at the entrances to grocery stores. I have had good response to small signs reading, WANTED: OLD OUTBOARD MOTOR. NEED NOT BE IN RUNNING CONDITION. There are a lot of people out there with old outboards that they do not want to have to demonstrate (since it is probably not in running condition) and who feel that they have few options for selling a non-running

Figure 02-04
You could scan the classified ads for weeks and not see as many old outboards for sale as you will see at one outboard motor swap meet.

Figure 02-05
Smaller meets are often held at private homes. Obviously this is a dry meet; no one wants to go boating in this kind of weather.

outboard. If you specify that it must be "running," or "late model" or a particular brand, you will probably get little response, and what engines you are called about will be priced high. If, however, you do not require the owner to demonstrate it, or even properly identify it, your odds of getting calls increase dramatically. You would be surprised at the number of people who know they have an outboard motor but know next to nothing about it, which is why you probably do not want to specify that you are only interested in OMC outboards. You may get a call from someone with a nice full-gearshift Brooklure who hasn't a clue that it is a close cousin to a Johnson or Evinrude. And it wouldn't hurt you to go look at other brands of old outboards; just don't buy them. Other sources of old outboards are friends, relatives, work associates, etc: spread the word that you are "into" old outboards. Chances are someone you know has an old outboard they are looking to get rid of.

Once you have located an old OMC outboard, then you must evaluate its condition

and arrive at a value. The only certain way to accurately evaluate an old outboard's condition is with a "tear-down," meaning a complete disassembly and inspection. Of course, you don't have the time or knowledge to do that, and the seller wants to know *now* if you are going to take the thing off his hands, so I will explain my procedures for making a quick inspection and evaluation of an outboard. I will say right here that there are problems that can be missed and that on occasion I have ended up with a lemon, and there is every possibility that you could as well. The way I protect myself in that situation is to be sure the engine is of a model I have a definite interest in acquiring, so that if it turns out to be junk, I can use it as a source of parts for a better example that (hopefully) I will run across in the future. I also offer a low price and stick to it; I would rather walk away without an outboard than to feel that I overpaid for a dud.

The first thing I do when examining an outboard is to grab the starter rope and give it a pull; if the engine refuses to rotate it might

Figure 02-06
Snow cover doesn't slow the "wheel'n & deal'n." At left is a 12 HP Gale Buccaneer; at right is an Evinrude 7½

Figure 02-07
A wet meet is a meet on the water where boats can be run. There will still be plenty of selling and swapping but with the added element of boating.

mean that the engine is "frozen" or "locked up," i.e., the pistons are stuck in the cylinders. If this is truly the case, the engine is probably only good for parts. An engine can "freeze up" due to corrosion resulting from improper storage. It is also possible that the engine overheated on its last outing or maybe was run without oil being mixed with the gasoline, as nearly all 2-cycle engines lacking oil injection require. Whatever the cause, I would advise avoiding a frozen engine unless you need some parts from it. A frozen engine is worth very little except when it is in very, very good cosmetic condition or if it has some rare parts on it, such as a 1950s Johnyrude 18 HP fitted with electric start (for some reason, there is a big demand for electric start on outboards, so the electric starter and related parts have value.)

But don't assume that an outboard is frozen if you cannot pull the starter rope; it might just be that the recoil starter has issues, and a recoil starter is usually a much simpler fix. Remove the cowling and try to manually rotate the flywheel in a clockwise direction. (Rotating the flywheel in a counterclockwise

direction can damage the water impeller.) If the starter rope won't move, but the flywheel turns, the problem is in the starter. Some models are fitted with a safety interlock to prevent starting in gear, another item to check. Although a recoil starter with a minor problem may not be sufficient reason to reject the engine, it is certainly reason to negotiate the price down a bit.

The "compression" of an engine is the amount of pressure, usually measured in pounds per square inch (PSI) that the piston generates in its cylinder as it travels up toward the cyclinder head. You can measure the cylinder pressure of an outboard with a compression gauge and learn what the compression is, but then no one will tell you what the compression *should* be. Compression figures are rarely specified in the service manuals, as if they are some sort of proprietary information. About all the manufacturers will tell you is that all cylinders of an engine should measure

Figure 02-08
Boat at the dock is powered by a 1920s outboard, while the boat getting underway was built by the driver who also restored the beautiful 1950s Mercury outboard powering it.

within about 10 to 15 percent of each other. An engine with cylinders with dramatically different readings has a problem.

A 2-cycle engine (which all old OMC outboards are) has a second "compression" that a 4-cycle engine does not have; crankcase compression. The fuel/air mixture is drawn from the carburetor into the crankcase of a two-cycle engine by the vacuum caused by the piston moving upwards, and then this mixture is forced through passages in the combustion chamber above the piston as the piston moves down. While the mixture is in the crankcase, oil mixed in with the gasoline lubricates the crankshaft and connecting rods. If insufficient compression is generated in the crankcase, the engine will run poorly or not at all. This crankcase compression is difficult to measure and most often you must eliminate all other potential sources of trouble to isolate a crankcase compression problem, unless you

Figure 02-09
Classic 1950s boats and outboards lined up at the dock. A wet meet provides you the opportunity to actually see these old outboards run.

get lucky and find evidence of a leak. For example, oil all over the top of the engine and the magneto may indicate a leaking upper crankcase seal.

Rather than taking to time to hook up a pressure gauge, I usually pull the starter rope several times and if the motor responds with a solid-sounding "thunk-thunk," I assume the compression is good. And most of the time it is (but not always; the gauge is the only sure method). If you pull the starter rope and get a "clunk-clunk," that is bad and the engine may have internal damage.

Figure 02-10
A classic aluminum Feathercraft boat powered by a 1957 Evinrude 35 HP Big Twin heads out for a run.

Figure 02-11
Outboards lined up for sale. Prices are marked on each and are often open to negotiation.

The next thing I check is the lower unit, or "bottom end" of the outboard, where the propeller is attached. The lower unit is a "right-angle" gearbox containing oil- or grease-lubricated gears. If the outboard motor has a forward-neutral-reverse gearshift, this is where the related mechanism is located. It is a fact of life that lower units on old outboard motors leak. The older OMC engines that I am recommending you look for almost all used a "two-piece" housing that is inherently difficult to keep sealed. Add years of wear on shafts and seals and maybe a bit of warping of housings and it is just a safe bet that most of these lower units will leak. What you want to verify is that no water has been left in the lower unit which could freeze during cold water, cracking the lower unit. Carefully inspect the lower unit housing for cracks of any sort. While it may be possible to patch a cracked lower unit with epoxy or by welding, the crack dramatically lowers the value of an old outboard. The cost

of a new replacement housing, if it is even available, would be prohibitive, and good used housings are also expensive as they are in demand. Also, keep in mind that the two-piece lower units housings were machined as a matched pair, which means that you should really not replace one half of the housing with a piece from another housing. Avoid motors with mismatched lower unit housings.

Assuming no lower unit cracks are found, it is a good idea to place the engine in an upright position and remove the oil drain screw from the bottom of the lower unit to see if any water drains out. The presence of water, even if the lower unit shows no cracks, is a sign of poor maintenance and should be used to bargain the price downward. A large regular-head screwdriver and a drain pan will be needed in order to check the lower unit. There are two of these large screws on the lower unit; the lower one is the drain while the upper one is the vent, and on some lower units they are so labeled.

Be aware that there is a third screw on the

Figure 02-12
More outboards and even a couple of electric trolling motors.

Figure 02-13
White engine in foreground is a 1962 Johnson 10 long shaft (20-inch); engine in back and to the right is a similar year Evinrude 10 HP short shaft (15-inch). Both engines were tagged at $150.00 and neither sold at that price. The Evinrude was in really nice cosmetic condition. Strangely enough, the grungy-looking Mercury behind the white Johnson did sell. The collectors at these meets will not necessarily be interested in the same engines that you are.

lower units of full gear shift engines, way down near the bottom of the lower unit. It is usually smaller than the vent and drain screws and usually has a Phillips head. You do *not* want to remove this smaller screw as it is the pivot pin for a bell crank that works the shift mechanism. If by chance you mistakenly remove a small screw from the lower unit of an OMC shift lower unit and the screw has a long "tail" on it, immediately try to reinstall the screw and do *not* touch the shift lever. Moving the shift lever can move the bell crank out of position. If the shifter has moved, the screw can be reinstalled but the shift mechanism will not function. Needless to say it is not ethical practice to intentionally disable the shift mechanism and use that to negotiate a cheaper price!

Water allowed to remain in the lower unit over an extended period of time can cause other damage as well. The shafts and gears within the lower units of many old outboards are ordinary steel and subject to corrosion. Old OMC outboards of 25 HP or more usually have roller and ball bearings in the lower

units which are subject to corrosion and wear, although they have the advantage of being replaceable. The bearings in smaller OMCs are usually bronze bushings, often cast integral with the housings. They are much less susceptible to damage by corrosion but they can not be replaced unless you are willing to have extensive machining done. OMC recommended replacing the entire lower unit housings if the cast-in-place bushings became worn.

Something else to look for on the lower unit are obvious signs of a very recent lower unit oil change, indicating that the owner may have prepped the engine in anticipation of selling it.

After writing several paragraphs expounding the evils of water in the lower unit, I have

Figure 02-14
Two old Johnson 5s; the one on the left is a late 1940s model TD-20 while the one on the right is an early 1950s TN-27 (basically a TD-20 with a neutral clutch added). These are a bit older than I would recommend for the cheap outboard buyer; virtually no new parts available and they are a bit strange.

Figure 02-15
Evidence that one man's garbage is another man's gold; someone bought this pile of stuff.

to say that most of these old lower units allow water to leak in. It is fairly rare to find one totally water-tight. What you are hoping to find is a lower unit that has had frequent oil changes as compensation for the leaking. This is how I deal with minor to moderate leaking of the lower units on my personal engines.

The condition of the propeller is important. While new propellers and even decent used propellers are available for the engines that we are looking at, the need for a new propeller should be figured into the price paid for the outboard. With the spark plug wires removed

from the spark plugs to ensure there is no possibility of the engine accidentally starting, rotate the propeller by hand with the engine in neutral (for those engines with a gearshift) and look for signs that the propeller shaft is bent (wobbling propeller/ strange wear patterns on propeller hub).

Also, shift the engine into forward and reverse as you slowly rotate the prop by hand. The nature of the shift mechanism is that an outboard will not shift fully into gear unless the prop or crankshaft is rotating so be sure to slowly turn the propeller as you try to shift it, and you should feel the engine shift solidly into both forward and reverse gear. Do not attempt to force an outboard into gear if the propeller or the power head is not turning as you may bend the linkage. Once you feel the gears engage, give the prop an extra hard turn to see if the engine is solidly in gear. The failure of the engine to fully engage forward *or* reverse may be caused by a minor linkage misadjustment or may be caused by major dam-

Figure 02-16
OMC pressurized fuel tanks are a common sight at swap meets; this particular example looked to be in pretty good shape and had the hose and quick connector for attaching to the motor. At $25.00 it was a bargain, even through it was missing the special cap. Comparable tanks (with cap) sell for well over $100.00 on the online auction sites (plus shipping).

Figure 02-17
Here is a plastic bag of pressure tank quick connectors for sale at $20.00 each. Not a real bad price if you need one (I have paid $20.00 for one I really needed.)

age. Failure to engage forward *and* reverse is probably a linkage problem (remember that little pivot screw on the lower unit?) but could also be major damage. You are assuming an additional risk with an engine that exhibits shift problems, so adjust you offering price accordingly, assuming you want to take that risk. And don't assume that an engine that appears to shift okay when the propeller is turned by hand will also shift correctly when under power; it is just that the likelihood of such a problem is somewhat reduced.

As mentioned previously, virtually all OMC-built outboard motors of up to 40 HP, built from the early 1950s until the late 1960s (at least) used magneto coils (ignition coils) that crack over time. It would be in your best interest to check them to see if they are

cracked, and a regular-head screwdriver is about the only tool needed. Remove the cowling of the engine, then remove the recoil starter from the top of the engine (usually held on by three screws). There will usually be a "cover plate" over a small hole in the top of the flywheel. Remove the cover plate and look through it while slowly turning the flywheel. You should see two cylindrical plastic things, located 180 degrees apart. If they are cracked, they need to be replaced. No big deal, but as it will cost you some money and some labor, use it to negotiate the price. By the way, cracked coils may still provide a spark at the spark plug, but don't count on that to continue when you are out on the water and a long way from help. Cracked coils have little if any remaining life in them.

You will notice I have said nothing about "checking for spark," which all the mechanics tell you to check for when evaluating an old engine. They will tell you to remove a spark plug and ground it against the engine and then

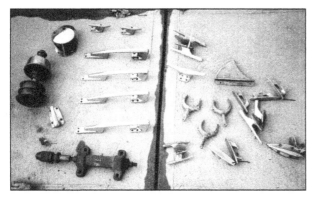

Figure 02-18
I bought a box containing all of this hardware for $10.00. I have even purchased sailboat hardware at an outboard motor swap meet. You just never know what someone will bring to sell.

Figure 02-19
People have hauled in outboards and parts by the trailer-load. The big engine on the stand over to the left is a Homelite 55 HP 4-cycle outboard from the 1960s; 4-cycle outboards are nothing new.

crank-over the engine to see if you can see, hear, or feel a spark at the spark plug. I don't waste my time checking old OMCs for spark. Any old engine that I am going to use is going to get treated to new ignition points, condensers, spark plug wires, spark plugs, and if they are cracked, new magneto coils as well. Other than the coils, all of these parts are considered tune-up items that should be replaced if they have never been, or if it has been years since they were last replaced. This is all low-dollar stuff that is as easy on the wallet as it is easy to install, and will give you an engine with a virtually new ignition system. So why bother checking the old ignition system?

Give the engine a good look-over: Does it appear to have all of its parts? Are all of the control knobs in place? Missing knobs may not seem like a big deal, but an engine with all of its knobs has most likely received better care than one that is missing knobs and maybe pieces of the cowlings.

Any signs of physical damage? Is the skeg (fin) on the very bottom of the lower unit bro-

ken or bent, indicating that the engine hit something? Are other chunks of metal broken off, indicating that the engine may have been dropped or otherwise abused?

Pull the starter rope out; does it look frayed and worn to the point where it might break? If the recoil starter rope appears to be almost new, how smoothly does it rewind? If the rope was replaced because the old rope broke during an attempt to start the engine, the recoil starter may have rewound violently, damaging the recoil spring, which may now bind and drag when the starter is operated. A conscientious owner would have replaced the rope *before* it broke, while a semi-conscientious owner would have replaced both the broken rope and the recoil starter spring. How conscientious do you think the former owners were?

Are there signs that the outboard has been used in saltwater, i.e., excessive corrosion? If at all possible I would suggest avoiding outboards that show signs of being used in salt water as the damage caused by failure to thoroughly flush the engine with fresh water after each use can be extensive. The old outboards were made of corrosion-prone die-cast aluminum and mild steel, and salt deposits can plug cooling water passages and lead to overheating. If you live far from the coasts you will probably see very few saltwater-damaged outboards but keep in mind that people move all the time and take their outboards with them. So you can not safely assume that an outboard in Chicago has never seen saltwater. Obviously those who live in coastal areas will need to be very vigilant. Avoid these engines if you can.

Remember that without a total disassembly (which I have never done when buying an old outboard) it is very difficult to totally evaluate the condition of an old outboard motor. The simple truth is that you are taking some risk. Keeping the amount of your investment to a minimum is about the only sure way to limit the amount of risk you are assuming. And focusing on one model or one series of outboard will allow you to use any junk outboard you mistakenly buy, as a parts engine for a better specimen. There are no guarantees with old outboard motors; if you feel you need a guarantee, you really need to look at either a new outboard or a late-model used outboard from a dealer. The buyer of an old outboard has to be willing to accept some risk.

Keep in mind that there are lots of old outboards laying around, so don't be in a hurry to buy the first one you see. Don't be afraid to turn one down if you think it has problems or if you think it is overpriced.

Figure 02-20
They usually feed you pretty well at these meets. Often there will be a donation jar to help pay for the lunch, which may just be hot dogs or may be a feast such as at this one. Other than that there is generally no admission charge. A great place to meet some interesting people and learn more about old outboard motors. These swap meets are held all over the USA (and in a few other countries) all throughout the year. An event calendar can be found at the web site of the Antique Outboard Motor Club, Inc (www.aomci.org)

3

Tools Needed, and Where to Begin

~

Once you have your obsolete OMC outboard, you are going to need a few tools in order to work on it. Not a whole lot of tools are required for repairing old OMC outboards: the minimum would be a good set of combination open-end/box-end wrenches in SAE sizes ("inch" measurements; not that silly metric stuff), a few good screwdrivers in both regular and Phillips types, and a good pair of needlenose pliers. Although not absolutely essential, a socket set would be very useful. A set of feeler gauges for setting the point gap is needed but only costs a few dollars.

About the only special tool required is a flywheel puller, needed to remove the flywheel as the ignition components are underneath it (03-01). While a genuine outboard motor fly-

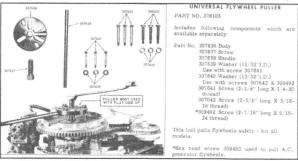

Figure 03-01
The factory flywheel puller is a nice tool, but pricey. You can get by much cheaper.

wheel puller is nice to have, any solidly constructed puller with a "three leg" yoke, such as a harmonic balancer puller or maybe a steering wheel puller, will probably work. I use an imported harmonic balancer puller that currently costs about $15.00 or less (03-02).

Use of puller will be covered in more detail in the chapter on magnetos. Another very handy tool to have is a torque wrench, which

Figure 03-02
The imported (made in China) puller that I have used for several years. You can get these from the online or local dealers of cheap imported tools. A trip to your local hardware store will probably be necessary to pick up screws that will fit the threaded holes in the flywheel.

Chances are the threads are ¼"-20, but may be 5/16"-18 or 5/16"-24. Try the ¼"-20 first. That's ¼-inch diameter and 20 threads per inch, in case you did not know. You will need three bolts about 2½ inches long, and pick up half a dozen ¼-inch washers while at the hardware store to use under the heads of the bolts.

45

tells you exactly how tight you are tightening bolts and nuts. Since some of the torque specifications (see Appendix, p.175) are given in "foot-pounds" and some are given in "inch-pounds," a wrench that reads both ranges would be nice; otherwise, pick up two cheap torque wrenches, one calibrated in foot-pounds and one in inch-pounds. My torque wrenches are ultra-cheap versions purchased through a discount tool store. Although not most accurate, they sure beat not having a torque wrench at all! One other item that comes in handy is an impact driver (03-03); I'm not talking about an air-operated impact wrench here, folks; this is a $15.00 thing that

Figure 03-04
The import tool sellers also have impact drivers, usually for around fifteen bucks. I have been using the same cheap one for several years and it does the job.

you hit with a hammer and which makes short work of screws that have not been loosened in fifty years (03-04).

Beyond the above tools, little more is needed. Back in 1961, Johnson recommended that their dealers' service departments possess the tools listed in Figure 03-05, in addition to a few special OMC tools. As you are not running an outboard motor service shop, where time is money and efficiency determines the bottom line profit, and since you are most likely going to avoid major overhauls of engines, you can get by with fewer tools than listed and none of the special OMC tools.

You will need an engine stand. A sawhorse will work, although you may need to bolt an extension of some sort to it or the engine may be too close to the ground. Smaller engines can utilize a short chunk of 2 x 6 or 2 x 8 lumber clamped in a sturdy bench-mounted vise. Use

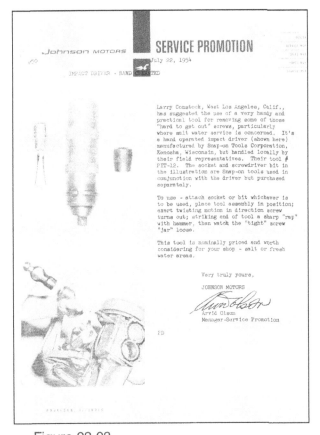

Figure 03-03
The factory recommended the Snap-On brand impact driver; a very nice tool but you probably cannot justify the price of Snap-On tools for your project.

your imagination to cobble up something solid; antique outboard motor collectors are known to frequent charity resale shops, buying up every senior citizen "walker" that they can find, which they then convert to outboard motor stands by simply bolting boards across the legs. Of course, you *could* just go out and buy a genuine factory-made outboard motor stand, but I think I know you pretty well by this point, and you're way too cheap for that!

A little paperwork would certainly come in handy. I mean a parts diagram (also referred to as a "parts list," "parts breakdown," or "exploded view") and a service manual. A reasonable substitute for a factory service manual would be one of the "generic" service manuals which cover many different brands and models of outboard motors, but in much less detail than a factory manual. One I can recommend is the *Old Outboard Motor Service Manual*, published by Intertec Publishing Corp. This particular manual comes in two volumes: Volume 1 covers engines of under 30 HP, while Volume 2 covers engines of 30 HP and over. These manuals cover most brands of outboards from the early to mid-1950s until about 1969. Be sure to look for the "old" outboard service manual if you are dealing with a pre-1970 outboard as they also publish manuals for later-model outboards.

Clymer Publications (a division of Intertec) also publishes a really nice service manual covering Johnson and Evinrudes of up to 125 HP, from 1956 to 1972. As this manual, called the *Evinrude/Johnson Outboard Shop Manual* does not devote space to other brands of outboards as the Old Outboard Motor Service Manual does, it covers the OMC engines in greater detail. If

you really want a factory service manual, copies of those can usually be obtained from the Ken Cook Co. www.kencook.com/evinrudejohnsonmanuals. As for the parts diagram, a few postings on some of the antique outboard motor chat boards or discussion groups may turn up someone who can scan and email you one for free. I have scanned and e-mailed parts diagrams many times.

One other book that will be invaluable in your outboard motor search is *The Old Outboard Book* by Peter Hunn. This book, which has been reprinted several times since its initial printing in 1992, has listings by model number of virtually all U.S.-manufactured (and some imported) outboard motors from the early twentieth century up until about 1970. This book will be a big help in identifying just exactly what outboard motor you are looking for. You do not need to have the current edition, so it may be possible to buy a used copy from one of the internet used book sources. Note that all but the very first edition of this book have an old outboard motor price guide. But I would place little confidence in this price guide, as the prices were established by a very limited survey of collectors in a limited geographic area. Something I do agree with is that the price of an old outboard can be greatly affected by cosmetics; sometimes more so than by the mechanical condition. As already said, the value of an old outboard is determined by a willing buyer and a willing seller. In fact the Antique Outboard Motor Club will not allow one to post an asking price for an old outboard on either its online bulletin board or its printed classified advertisements. The club does not want such adds to serve as a de facto price guide.

Keep in mind that while it is certainly fine to purchase new copies of these books, they can often be found in public libraries or sometimes a used copy can be purchased from one of the online used book sources; I have had good luck dealing the Advanced Book Exchange, www.abebooks.com; and there are other online sources of used books as well, such as www.bookfinder.com. Nothing wrong with used books, although my publisher and I highly recommend that you purchase a *new* copy of this book!

You will probably need to buy some replacement parts and this is where selecting an OMC product really pays off. You can purchase parts through the local Johnson and Evinrude dealer, but there are alternatives. There is an after-market supplier of outboard motor parts called Sierra and they supply many of the parts needed for repairs of the scope that we will be discussing. Sierra parts can be purchased through just about any boat dealer, regardless of the brand of outboard the dealer carries. In fact, you might be better off purchasing Sierra parts for a Johnson or Evinrude through a dealer that does not sell Johnsons or Evinrudes, as those dealers will probably try to sell you OEM parts at a higher price. As of this writing, Sierra parts can also be purchased through NAPA auto parts stores although often the countermen are not aware of it, and most likely the parts will have to be ordered.

At this point you are probably wondering just where to start. Following is the sequence I

usually follow when rehabilitating one of these old engines. This procedure assumes that there is no major damage to the engine.

The first order of business should be to give the engine a good cleaning/degreasing. I have found that Castrol Super Clean, often found in the automotive departments of discount stores, does a good job of removing decades-old dirt and grease. It does an equally good job of removing decals and dulling the paint, so if you want to preserve the paint and decals on your engine, use something milder. I have sometimes used kitchen oven cleaner to remove baked-on grease from exhaust components, but as oven cleaner is rather caustic, it can damage aluminum if allowed to remain on the surface very long, and can remove paint if applied to the surface at all. Remove the cowling of the engine, and give the entire engine a good scrubbing with whatever cleaner you have chosen and a toothbrush or two. Rinse well with the garden hose but be careful to avoid spraying water into the carburetor or up into the magneto under the flywheel. Make sure that the spark plugs have their little ring-shaped gaskets and that they are tight, so that water does not enter the cylinders. Once clean, allow the engine to dry.

I usually begin the actual repairs by removing the flywheel and replacing the ignition points, condensers, spark plug wires, and spark plugs, and also the magneto coils if they are cracked. Others might suggest that if the engine has spark you need not worry about replacing these items, or if the engine does not have spark, that you should trouble-shoot the engine and try to determine exactly which part(s) need to be replaced. My opinion is that since these parts are easy and cheap to find for the engines that are the subject of this book, you can avoid a lot of headaches and frustration by just replacing it all in the beginning. The risk is that you may later find a major problem with the engine that renders it a parts motor after you have spent the time and money installing new parts. Your choice.

You check for spark by removing the spark plug wires from the spark plugs and then removing the spark plugs themselves, leaving the engine easy to spin because there is no compression with the spark plugs out. Put a spark plug wire on a spark plug and hold the plug up against a good metal ground. You want to ground the outer metal shell of the plug, not the bent center electrode, on the engine, then spin the engine with the recoil starter. It is a good idea to hold the plug with a rag or glove as you can get a pretty nasty shock if the ignition system is working. I usually clamp the spark plug to a metal portion of the engine with a pair of locking pliers such as Vise-Grips, which leaves both hands free to do the spinning. The result should be an audible snap and a visible spark at that center electrode. If you do not get a spark, check to be sure the spark plug is really grounded to the engine; make sure that the spark plug wire boot is firmly seated on the spark plug; try a different spark plug (maybe that plug is bad). If the engine has a "push to stop" kill switch, trace the wires between the switch and the magneto and you should find connectors in each wire that you can disconnect to isolate the switch from the system (kill switches have

been known to short out). If you still do not get a spark, chances are you are going to have to go into the magneto, but that is not a big deal (see Chapter 4).

Once the magneto is torn-down, I then remove the carburetor, disassemble and clean it, and reassemble it with a rebuild kit (see Chapter 5). Chances are the carb needs cleaning anyway, and the soft parts in the rebuild kit (gaskets, etc.) are resistant to the alcohol in today's gasoline. The existing parts may not be. For the same reason, new fuel hoses are in order. Although genuine marine hose is the best (and you only need a few feet of it) I have used plenty of automotive fuel hose with few ill effects. This should not be taken as an indication that you should do the same.

If your engine has a fuel pump, you will have to decide whether to use the pump as is (assuming it still pumps) or to replace it. Most of the fuel pumps on the smaller OMC engines in the era we are concerned with were not considered rebuildable by OMC and so no rebuild kits were offered. I have heard stories of people who have made new diaphragms for their pumps out of rubber (possibly Buna rubber from a gasket shop) but I don't know if I would bother. If the old pump still works, I go ahead and use it as-is, but am always mindful that it may not have much life left in it.

With the carb. rebuilt and reinstalled, and the magneto back on the engine and producing a good spark, I usually turn attention to the water pump impeller. I strongly advise replacing that impeller; I have seen, several times, an old impeller last just long enough to get the boat out to the middle of the lake or river and then fail. Although I might someday be tempted to skip the magneto and carb work, I will *always* replace the pump impeller. To try to get a little more life out of an old impeller is false economy that might just cost you your engine.

The rope on the recoil starter should also get a critical examination and be replaced if there is any doubt as to its condition. Since the recoil starter springs for most of these old OMC engines are fairly cheap, I often replace that as well.

Finally, changing the oil in the lower unit is always a good idea, and if you know that you are starting with fresh oil, if water turns up in the oil you will know that it wasn't already in there.

The above items should be done to just about any engine you end up with; additional work may be necessary depending upon the condition of the engine you buy. The goal is to find an engine that requires no more than the above work.

```
JOHNSON MOTORS SERVICE
   TOOL SET #JM-82B
 1 each of the following

Combination wrench 5/16"        Standard screwdriver impact socket
Combination wrench 3/8"         Phillips socket #2
Combination wrench 7/16"        Phillips socket #3
Combination wrench 1/2"         Adapter 3/8" to 1/2" drive
Combination wrench 9/16"
Combination wrench 5/8"         Allen wrench set
Combination wrench 11/16"       Adjustable wrench 10"
Combination wrench 3/4"
Combination wrench 13/16"       Pliers 7"
                                Diagonal cutters 7"
Torquemeter 600 inch - lbs.     Duck bill pliers
Torquemeter 150 feet - lbs.     Battery terminal pliers
                                Interlocking joint pliers 9"
Socket 3/16" - 3/8" drive       Hose clamp pliers"
Socket 3/8"  - 3/8" drive
Socket 7/16" - 3/8" drive       Standard screwdriver 2"
Socket 1/2"  - 3/8" drive       Standard screwdriver 6"
Socket 9/16" - 3/8" drive       Standard screwdriver 12"
Socket 5/8"  - 3/8" drive       Phillips screwdriver #2
Socket 11/16"- 3/8" drive       Phillips screwdriver #3
Socket 3/4"  - 3/8" drive
Socket 13/16"- 3/8" drive       Screw starter
Socket 7/8"  - 3/8" drive
                                Pin punch 3/32"
Spark plug socket               Pin punch 5/32"
                                Pin punch 5/16"
Sliding "T" handle, 3/8" drive  Center punch
Speeder 3/8" drive              Flat chisel
Ratchet 3/8" drive
Nut spinner 3/8" drive          Ball peen hammer - 4 oz.
                                Ball peen hammer - 12 oz.
Extension - 6"                  Rawhide hammer  - 2 1/2 lbs.
                                Rawhide mallet  - 1/2 lb.
Universal joint                 Flywheel holder
                                Piston ring spreader
Standard screwdriver socket     Starter current indicator
Allen socket 3/8"
Allen socket 7/32"              Tool chest with tumber lock as shown.
Allen socket 5/16"

Sliding "T" handle, 1/2" drive
Socket 1 5/16" (For flywheel nuts)

Throttle control wrench
Powerhead takedown nut wrench

Impak driver
Impact socket 3/8"
Impact socket 7/16
Impact socket 1/2"
Impact socket 9/16"
```

Figure 03-05
The factory-recommended tool list, not including some special OMC tools. Unless you are opening an outboard motor repair shop, you can get by with a lot less than this, but notice that there is nothing really unusual about the tools on this list. You probably already own a good portion of them, and any of this that you buy will eventually prove useful in projects beyond boats and outboard motors.

4

The Ignition System

Your old OMC outboard came from the factory with old-fashioned points and condenser ignition. This means that the spark plugs get their spark from a very reliable system of very inexpensive components. Unlike modern electronic ignition, where a single "black box" can cost hundreds of dollars, your old outboard can be given what amounts to a virtually new ignition system for well under a hundred dollars, even if the magneto coils are cracked; if you get lucky and find an engine that already has new coils, your parts costs will probably be under fifty dollars.

For the reader not conversant in low-tech, ignition points are little mechanical switches which are opened and closed by a cam on the crankshaft and signal the sparkplug when to spark. A condenser is a little metal tube with a wire coming out of it, and it is basically a short-term storage device for electric current—it stores an electrical charge for a fraction of a second. These descriptions are simplified, but just remember that points and condensers for the old outboards I recommend here are very easy to get and very cheap.

A tune-up kit consisting of two sets of points and two condensers (a set for each of the two cylinders), will set you back less than twenty bucks. Changing out points and condensers is a breeze; merely a matter of removing some screws and a few wires, and since there are two of everything on these twin-cylinder engines, you can work on one side while leaving the other as a guide—like a built-in 3-D parts diagram!

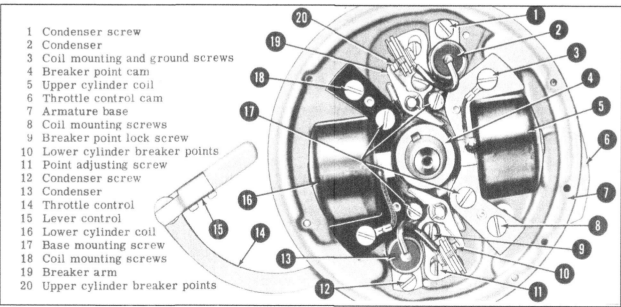

1 Condenser screw
2 Condenser
3 Coil mounting and ground screws
4 Breaker point cam
5 Upper cylinder coil
6 Throttle control cam
7 Armature base
8 Coil mounting screws
9 Breaker point lock screw
10 Lower cylinder breaker points
11 Point adjusting screw
12 Condenser screw
13 Condenser
14 Throttle control
15 Lever control
16 Lower cylinder coil
17 Base mounting screw
18 Coil mounting screws
19 Breaker arm
20 Upper cylinder breaker points

Figure 04-01

This magneto, with only minor variations, was used in all 2-cylinder OMC-built outboard motors from 1951 until the early 1970s.

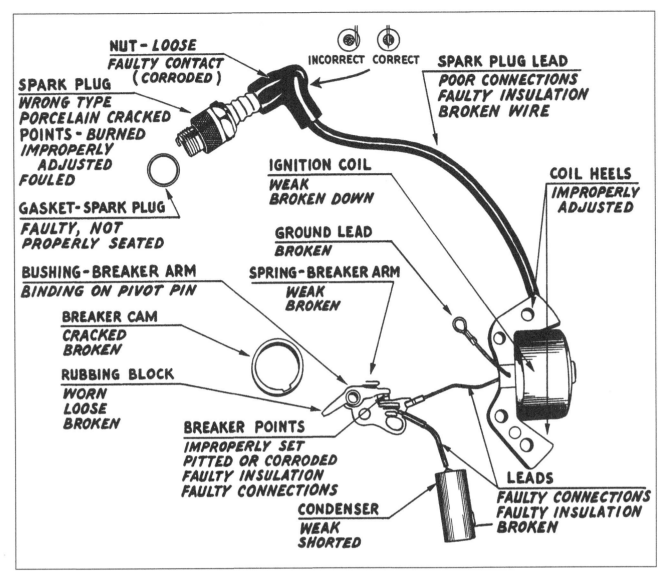

Figure 04-02
Except for the magnet embedded in the flywheel, this is the entire ignition system for one cylinder. Everything (except the breaker cam) will be duplicated for the second cylinder. The beauty of an old fashioned points-and-condenser ignition system is that little in the way of sophisticated test gear is needed to trouble-shoot such a system and replacement parts for these old OMC engines are readily available and cheap.

From 1951 until the early 1970s OMC used essentially the same magneto for all of its 2-cylinder outboards with only minor variations between them, so if you have worked on the magneto of a 3 HP model, you will feel right at home dealing with the "mag" on a 40 (Figure 04-01).

Note that no outside source of electricity (i.e. a battery) is needed for the engine to run;

that is one of the beauties of a magneto ignition system.

Besides the points and condensers, the magneto (ignition system) on these engines consists of a coil, magnets encased within the rim of the flywheel, a spark plug wire, and a spark plug. That is all there is to a magneto that will fire one cylinder. Since nearly all of the engines we are talking about have two cylinders, this stuff is all duplicated for the second cylinder.

What can go wrong? Well, points can become burned and pitted due to arcing; condensers can short out, either internally or to their outside metal cases. Insulation on spark plug wires can go bad, or the inner wire may break. There are ways to test points and condensers: you can use a simple home-made test light to see if the points are making and breaking contact, and the same test light can be used to check a condenser for a short between the wire and the case (a special tester is needed to check for an internal short in a condenser.) (Figure 04-02).

But why bother? I always replace the points and condensers on these old OMC engines. It saves time and hassle, and costs little. I recommend that you do so, too. While you're at it, it would not hurt to replace the spark plug wires as well. New copper-core plug wire is not too expensive and you only need a few feet of it. Don't buy the graphite core wire which is commonly used in electronic ignition systems.

Now to removing the flywheel. One of the few specialized tools you need to work on these engines is a flywheel puller. The one that I use was made in China by political prisoners and was sold as a cheap automotive harmonic balancer puller. About ten years old, mine originally cost under ten $10.00. Often such things as steering wheel pullers can be used. The main thing to consider is that the puller must use the three threaded holes on the top of the flywheel, and not lift on the rim on the flywheel. The puller's three legs screw into the three flywheel holes, and the center threaded mandrel (rod) bears on the top of the crankshaft poking out the center of the flywheel.

Loosen the flywheel nut (a big strap wrench helps to hold the flywheel from turning while wrenching on the nut) and back it off a few turns but do not remove it. Leave the nut above the level of the flywheel so the center mandrel (big threaded center post) of the puller bears against both the crankshaft and the nut. The three threaded legs should fully engage the threads in the holes in the flywheel, but keep in mind that if the screws extend very far below the level of the flywheel, they may damage the coils. For that reason it is best not to allow the flywheel to turn while putting tension on the puller (Figure 04-03 & 04-04).

Once the puller is on, fully threaded, and square to the flywheel (in line with the crankshaft), you can start screwing down the mandrel and putting tension on the flywheel. I use a second wrench or a large screwdriver on the puller to keep the flywheel from rotating. Just how much tension you can safely apply without fear of stripping the threads out of the three flywheel holes is anyone's guess. You are going to have to make a judgment. If you strip those holes, or damage the top of the crankshaft, you have problems. A little penetrating oil on the crankshaft threads might help, along with heat from a propane torch. If you lift up on the flywheel, you will notice a bit of end-play, i.e. the crankshaft moves up and down a very slight amount. You can pull up on the flywheel (*not* the armature plate underneath it), and give the puller a smart and square smack with a hammer. Lifting up the flywheel will allow the crankshaft a bit of downward travel which might be enough to break it loose from the crankshaft taper.

EVINRUDE
Service Bulletin

Service Department
EVINRUDE MOTORS
Milwaukee 16, Wisconsin

BIG TWIN – LARK
NUMBER 40.-3
DECEMBER 21, 1959

FLYWHEEL REMOVAL – 40 H.P. LARK II

You were recently advised of the availability of the newly designed Universal flywheel puller (Service Bulletin No. M-347).

The following is the suggested procedure for removing the flywheel on the 40 H.P. Lark II with the new puller.

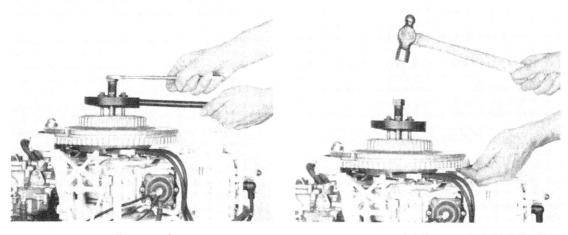

Figure 1   Figure 2

1. Remove the flywheel nut.

2. Turn the large center screw of the puller to its outer limit. Attach puller to flywheel, using 3 special hardened screws with washers. (Be sure screws are completely threaded into flywheel.)

3. Turn large center screw until it contacts the crankshaft and tighten securely with a wrench (Fig. 1).

4. While holding up on the rim of the flywheel (Fig. 2) strike puller screw sharply with a hammer. If flywheel does not loosen, repeat steps 3 and 4. (Note - lifting the flywheel rim is very important, it will absorb the hammer shock and prevent damage to the power-head.)

   The procedure in step 4 is required on the 40 H.P. model, due to the 100-105 ft. lb. flywheel nut torque on assembly. Note - the 40 H.P. Lark engines are equipped with a new strengthened flywheel, utilizing a forged steel hub. With the new hub, it is possible for hairline cracks to appear between puller screw holes, however, these will in no way effect strength and should be disregarded.

Figure 04-03   How the factory recommended that the flywheel be removed. . . .

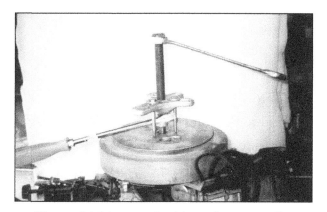

Figure 04-04 . . . And how I remove fly-wheels—pretty close to the factory method but with cheaper tools. Flywheel puller in place on the flywheel: the three small bolts have been threaded completely into the flywheel, taking care not to allow them to extend excessively below the underside of the flywheel where they could damage the magneto components. The orange-handled screwdriver is used to prevent the fly-wheel from turning as the mandrel (large center screw of the puller) is tightened, although the proper tool for the job would be a large strap wrench which fits around the whole flywheel.

Don't hammer on the puller unless you are lifting up on the flywheel and making this slack available, and don't hammer directly on the crankshaft! Also, be aware that hammer blows can reduce the magnetism in the flywheel magnets. With enough tension and penetrating oil and heat and tapping, the flywheel will eventually come loose with a bang that will convince you that something has broken. Remove the flywheel and you are now looking at your magneto (Figure 04-05).

As mentioned, if the coils are cracked, replace them. New ones can be found for under twenty bucks each with a little searching; otherwise, as of this writing coils cost about $25.00 each at an outboard dealer. It is necessary to remove the armature plate (round

Figure 04-05
Flywheel has been removed, revealing cracks in the purple and white magneto coils, a common problem. The magneto will need to come off the engine to replace the coils and the spark plug wires. If just the points and condensers needed replacing, the magneto could stay right where it is. Although these coils are purple, they also came in red, green, blue, and maybe a few other colors as well.

plate the stuff is mounted on) from the engine to replace coils. There is usually a clip to disconnect the throttle linkage from the plate (#15 on Figure 4.1), and the armature plate is held down with four screws (#17, Figure 4.1), two of which pass through the coil laminations. Before removing the armature plate, make note of how it is positioned on the engine; when it comes time to reinstall it, you don't want it to be rotated 180 degrees out of position. A few photos might serve as an excellent reference when you later reassemble the engine (Figure 04-06).

Can coils that are not cracked be bad? Sure they can, it just does not happen very often.

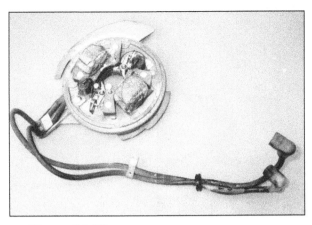

Figure 04-06
Magneto removed from the engine. It is not necessary for you to understand electromagnetic theory in order to work on this thing. If would be a good idea to make some notes and take a few photos to be sure you can put it back together the way it was.

Figure 04-07
The underside of the magneto.

Since about any old outboard engine can benefit from new points, condensers, and spark plug wires, all of which are cheap, I would replace those items first. If you still have one cylinder with no spark, you might try substituting time and labor for cash and swapping the positions of the coils to see if the live and dead cylinders have also swapped positions.

The spark plug wires are attached to the coils by merely pushing them into the opening and onto a pointed stud. The spark plug wires are held to the underside of the armature plate with various clips that will need to be removed in order to withdraw the old wires and install the new wires. I highly recommend that you take careful notes and a few more photos of the underside of the armature plate before removing parts from it. Most armature plates are used on several different models of engines, so there are extra holes that may not be used in your particular engine but which will serve to confuse you when it is time to put it all back together (Figure 04-08).

You might also want to keep track of which spark plug wire goes to which cylinder. Usually the upper wire is marked with a small metal band that says "up." Should you lose track even after having been warned, keep in mind

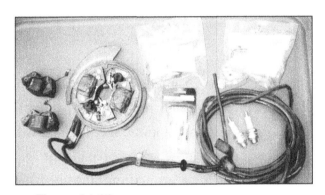

Figure 04-08
All needed parts on hand. Plastic bags contain two new Sierra #18-5181 coils; there are also two used coils salvaged from a "dead" engine. There is a few feet of new metallic-core spark plug wire, a couple of new spark plugs, and a Sierra tune-up kit consisting of two sets of points and two sets of condensers; one kit only is needed for these 2-cylinder engines.

that the starboard breaker points fire the lower cylinder through the rear coil while the port breaker points fire the upper cylinder through the front coil. I always reuse the old spark plug boots when installing new wires, unless the old boots are obviously damaged.

With the new parts on hand you are ready to begin replacing pieces one side at a time, leaving the other side intact to act as a guide (Figure 04-09). When installing the coils, attention must be paid to the "air gap," which

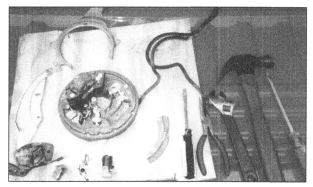

Figure 04-09
The old parts for one cylinder have been removed; the parts for the second cylinder remain intact to act as a guide. Shown are the tools being used (just kidding about the hammer).

basically means how close the magnets imbedded in the spinning flywheel should be to the laminated metal heels of the coils. Although there is a special tool made for this setting, it is certainly not needed (I have the tool but have never used it).

You will notice a small machined surface on the magneto plate directly below the coil heels. Basically the coil heels need to be flush with machined surface so that your fingers feel no noticeable step as you rub the area (04-10).

Once the new parts have all been installed on

the magneto, you can re-install the magneto on your engine. This is where your notes and photos will come in handy. Also note that you must hold back the little rocker arms on the points so that they do not hang up on the eccentric (cam) on the crankshaft as the magneto is installed. If you don't, you risk damaging the points. One last note is that some of these cams just sit on the crankshaft while some sit on a spring; the cams that sit on a spring can present additional challenges as the cam must be held down while you are also trying to hold back the points' rocker arms. It is just a matter of using your fingers.

Now you can set the points gap of .020" (#10 and #20, Fig. 04-01). Rotate the crankshaft until the rubbing block for that particular set of points (on the "leg" of the points) is aligned with the flywheel key, leaving the points at their most open setting, and use a feeler gauge to set the gap. The "gap" is a measurement of how wide the ignition points open up and it is a fairly critical measurement that is fairly easy to make. (Figure 04-11). Probably more important than the actual gap measurement, however, is that both sets of points have the same gap. On these old OMCs, the gap is almost always .020" so find the leaf of your cheap feeler gauge that is marked .020" and also find the leaves for the next size up (probably .022") and also the next size down (probably .018"). The gap on the points are adjusted with a regular-head screwdriver turning what appears to be a screw head (but actually is not) that moves the base of the points back and forth. This adjustment "screw" is actually an eccentric or cam and very little turning is

EVINRUDE
SERVICE BULLETIN

Service Department
EVINRUDE MOTORS
Milwaukee 16, Wisconsin

NUMBER 196
April 7, 1952

MAGNETO SUGGESTIONS

FLEETWIN—MODEL 4443-44   FASTWIN —MODEL 4441-42
MODEL 4447-48   BIG TWIN—MODEL 2001-02
LIGHTWIN—MODEL 3012-13   MODEL 2003-04

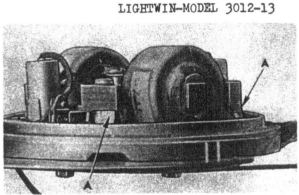

Figure 1

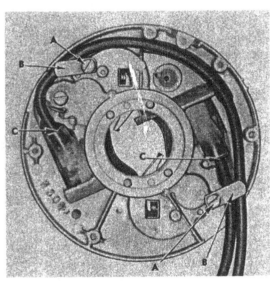

Figure 2

1. Installation of the coil assembly on the new armature plate is very simple--merely a matter of connecting all leads as provisions are made to accomplish the operation with necessary lead terminals and corresponding screws.

It is necessary to maintain distance or clearance between the coil heels and magnet pole shoes (on the flywheel). When installing the new coil draw the lamination mounting screws, Part #510195 (2 for each coil), up snugly, but not securely (at this time). Observe the machined bosses on the armature plate casting-"A" in figure 1. Tap lightly on coil heels until they come to rest "flush" with machined surfaces of the bosses. Tighten lamination mounting screws #510195 to secure the position of the coil assembly recheck to be sure they are flush with machined surfaces of the bosses.

2. No provision is made for soldering the high tension leads to coil #580118, as formerly required. A small needle like point is soldered to one end of the coil secondary (high tension). A satisfactory connection or contact is made by inserting the end of the high tension wire into the opening so that the sharp point is buried in the copper center of the high tension lead.

Before attempting to connect the wire, be sure to check to see that the needle point is in the center of the hole in the coil case. Attach the high tension lead after the coil has been mounted to the armature plate. Remove high tension cable clamp screw "A" and high tension lead clamp screw "B". (Figure 2).

Clip the end of the high tension lead off squarely. Then thrust the end of the lead into the opening as far as it will go, in order that the sharp point is buried in the copper center of the high tension lead. ("C" figure 2). Replace the high tension lead clamp and be sure to fasten the screw, holding the clamp, securely.

Figure 04-10
Instructions for installing the coils.

EVINRUDE
SERVICE BULLETIN

Service Department
EVINRUDE MOTORS
Milwaukee 16, Wisconsin

NUMBER 141
April 9, 1951

NEW ARMATURE PLATE

The armature plate illustrated is the one used currently on the models, 4443 Fleetwin, 4441 Fastwin, and the 2001 Big Twin. With the exception of handle and cam, this armature plate is the same for all 3 models.

The magnet rotor has been discontinued and is replaced by a magnet cast into the zinc flywheel. The breaker point cam is keyed to the crankshaft, consequently removeable if occasion requires.

The familiar push rod type of breaker point assembly has been replaced by a breaker arm arrangement on the order of that used on previous Evinrude motors.

This change means that to give complete service, it is necessary to stock only one armature plate assembly, with the three different armature handles and cams.

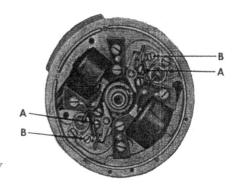

TO ADJUST THE MAGNETO BREAKER POINTS

Breaker point action is accomplished by a rubbing block attached to the breaker arm which rides or follows contour of the cam keyed to the crankshaft. Points break on the cam's high side, close on low side. Degree of breaker point opening (gap) is dependent on position of the stationary point with relation to action of the breaker arm. Thus, to obtain correct gap setting (.020'' full open) an arrangement is provided to permit ''pivoting'' of the entire breaker point assembly to correspondingly affect breaker action.

The breaker point assembly is anchored and held fast by screw ''A''.
Screw ''B'' is machined with an offset head (eccentric) which when turned to the left increases gap between the points; when turned right the gap closes. To adjust or set breaker point gap, turn crankshaft until rubbing block rides on highest point of breaker cam. This is IMPORTANT. Loosen anchor screw ''A'' slightly--just enough to permit pivoting of the bracket. Turn adjusting screw ''B'' to right or left as required. Check gap with .020'' feeler strip--retighten anchor screw ''A''. Repeat operation to adjust points for other cylinder. When checking ignition, always check and inspect both sets of coils, condenser, and points, if the engine is an alternate firing twin or four cylinder. Single or opposed twins have only one coil, condenser, and set of points.

If necessary, clean the breaker points by spreading carefully with blunt instrument to insert point dresser; then release spreader and work dresser up and down until surfaces are made smooth and clean. Insert strip of clean paper between points and in similar fashion remove traces of dressing material which may have adhered to point surfaces. The breaker points must be flat, smooth, and clean to realize utmost magneto performance.

Do not use emery cloth for this operation. If a point dresser is not available, fold a narrow strip of 00 sandpaper back to back in such a manner that it can be inserted between the points to clean or dress both surfaces simultaneously. It is advisable to break the rough edges first by rubbing sanded sides together. Be sure all traces of sand are removed on completion of this operation.

Cleaning or dressing in above manner is recommended only as an emergency measure. To insure maximum motor performance have new points installed at the first opportunity.

Note port provided in the flywheel for inspection, cleaning and adjusting of the breaker points. This operation may, however, be more thoroughly accomplished by removing the flywheel.

EVINRUDE MOTORS
Service Manager

Figure 04-11   Instructions for setting the gap of the ignition points.

Figure 04-12
The .020" leaf of your feeler gauge should fit between the points with just a slight bit of "drag." The .018" leaf should be very loose while the .022" leaf should not enter the gap without being forced (don't force it). Make sure that the rubbing block for the set of points that you are adjusting is lined up with the key on the crankshaft while making your adjustments.

required to make the adjustment (#11, Fig. 04-01). The full range of adjustment is available with just half a turn, so we are talking about very small adjustments. When the gap is set correctly the .020" leaf of the gauge should slide in between the points contacts with just a bit of resistance while the .022" should not want to enter the gap without the points contacts spreading apart more and the .018" should easily enter the gap.

And remember that both sets of points

should have the same gap even if the actual gap measurement is not exactly correct. You might loosen the screw which holds the base of the points slightly in order to make the adjustment a bit easier, but be sure to check and recheck the gap setting after re-tightening the mounting screw as that can cause the gap to change. And after you set both gaps, go back and re-check both gaps (Figure 04-12).

Set the flywheel on and rotate slowly clockwise to ensure noth'n is hitting noth'n. I have heard of more damage done to engines by people who did not pay attention to clearances and then hit the electric starter. Thoroughly read the service bulletins printed herein and check that the flywheel rotates freely at every step. It is important that the key on the crankshaft be properly positioned before tightening the flywheel nut, or you will risk damaging the flywheel or the crankshaft (04-13 & 04-14).

It is also important that you torque (tighten) the nut properly (Figure 04-15). An improperly tightened flywheel nut can cause the flywheel key to shear, causing the flywheel to slip to a different position on the crankshaft. If this happens, the timing of the ignition is incorrect and the engine probably will not run. Here's a hint; if you have just re-installed the flywheel and while test-running the engine it suddenly quits and will not restart, check to see if the flywheel key has sheared. A sheared key is not that big of a problem to replace, but occasionally the crankshaft keyway is damaged and that could be a big problem as can any damage to the crankshaft.

POWERHEAD 948

October, 1971

FLYWHEEL KEY INSTALLATION FOR 3, 4, 5, 5.5, 6, 7.5, 9.5, 15, 18, and 25 H.P.

When inserting the flywheel key into the crankshaft keyway of any engine listed above, be sure the single upset mark on the side of the key is facing down and the top surface of the key is parallel to the taper on the crankshaft as illustrated. Correct installation of the key is important, since it also engages and positions the cam in proper relationship with the crankshaft for precise ignition timing. This upset assures a tight fit between the key and the cam: therefore, if the key is incorrectly installed, the cam may become loose on the crankshaft resulting in incorrect ignition timing.

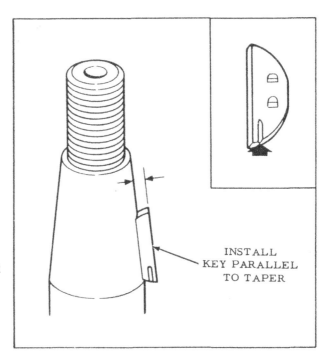

INSTALL
KEY PARALLEL
TO TAPER

EVINRUDE MOTORS

Service Department

Figure 04-13
When installing the flywheel, the key should be parallel to the tapered surface of the crankshaft. A damaged (bent) key can affect the ignition timing.

EVINRUDE
Service Bulletin

Service Department
EVINRUDE MOTORS
Milwaukee 16, Wisconsin

LARK II – BIG TWIN
NUMBER 40-5
FEBRUARY 22, 1960

FLYWHEEL KEY ASSEMBLY – 40 H.P. LARK II MODELS

Figure 1

Figure 2

Positive location of the flywheel key is necessary when assembling the flywheel in order to provide proper magneto timing. Positioning the key as
shown (Figure 1) before assembly, will insure proper fit of the key into the
flywheel hub key way for correct assembly.

It is possible to assemble the flywheel with the key located as shown
(Figure 2) so that the hub will ride on the key and not seat properly on the
crankshaft taper. The engine can be started, assembled in this manner, but
after a short period of running both flywheel and crankshaft will be
permanently damaged.

Always make sure that the key is positioned properly and that the flywheel
seats on the crankshaft taper before tightening the flywheel nut. NOTE: A
torque wrench must be used when tightening the flywheel nut to insure correct
assembly. Tighten to 1CO-105 ft. lbs.

EVINRUDE MOTORS

Richard Bayley

Service Promotion Manager

Richard Bayley
jw

Figure 04-14   Placement of the key in the crankshaft keyway can be critical on 1960 and 1961
40 HP models, as they had a reputation for shearing keys and breaking crankshafts. If you want a
40, the 1962 and later models were much improved.

EVINRUDE
Service Bulletin

Service Department
EVINRUDE MOTORS
Milwaukee 16, Wisconsin

NUMBER M-346
NOVEMBER 30, 1959

FLYWHEEL NUT TORQUE

As you know proper flywheel nut torque is extremely important on all engines to prevent the flywheel from becoming loose on the crankshaft taper. A loose flywheel will result in serious damage not only to the flywheel but to the crankshaft as well.

The factory recommended flywheel nut torque values for popular models are as follows:

HP	FT. LBS.	INCH LBS.	HP	FT. LBS.	INCH LBS.
3	30-40	360-480	25	60-65	720-780
5.5	40-45	480-540	30	60-65	720-780
7.5	40-45	480-540	35	60-65	720-780
10	40-45	480-540	40	100-105	1200-1260
15	40-45	480-540	50	70-85	840-1020
18	40-45	480-540	75	70-85	840-1020

NOTE! Torque values have been increased to 100-105 ft. lbs. on 40 H.P. Lark II models. This is very important and should be brought to the attention of all service personnel.

It is important that all flywheels be installed _dry_, this means that Methalene Chloride, or other suitable non-toxic solvents should be used to remove all traces of oil and grease from the crankshaft taper, the keyway and key, and the tapered flywheel hub before assembling.

EVINRUDE MOTORS

Richard Bayley

Richard Bayley
Service Promotion Manager

RB/jdb

Figure 04-15
The flywheel nut needs to be properly torqued; too loose and the flywheel may "fly" damaging itself and the crankshaft; too tight and you risk stretching the hub of the flywheel causing it to sit too low on the crankshaft and causing interference with the magneto. Wipe the taper clean of grease and oil before installing the flywheel.

Figure 04-16
Damage to flywheel hub caused when the flywheel nut loosened while the engine was running.

Figure 04-17
The crankshaft taper and keyways were also damaged. A sad fate for a 1940 Johnson.

Just in case you don't believe me that flywheel nut torque is a big deal, have a look at Figures 04-16 and 04-17. These are photos of what happened to my prized 1940 Johnson 22 HP outboard when I allowed the flywheel nut to loosen. While running at high speed on a beautiful summer day, the engine suddenly slowed and stopped. As the boat fell down off plane, I swiveled around in my seat to see the flywheel visibly wobbling on top of the engine. Thinking at first that I had broken the crankshaft, a quick inspection showed that the nut had loosened and the flywheel had "flown," destroying the flywheel hub and badly damaging the crankshaft taper and keyway in the process. This is major damage that only new parts (hard to find for a 1940 engine) or major machine shop work can repair.

The linkage between the armature plate and the carburetor throttle "butterfly" will eventually need to be connected and adjusted, but as the next chapter will deal with removing, cleaning, and rebuilding the carb, the linkage can be left until later. In fact, I usually leave the armature plate off the engine until after I have removed and reinstalled the carb. This leaves you a little more room to work.

One last comment before we move on: Should your engine have electric start, be very careful when wiring the starting circuit as an improperly wired starter switch can feed 12 volts into your brand-new coils, which will cause them to explode (in a minor way), destroying them (Form 04-18).

EVINRUDE
Service Bulletin

Service Department
EVINRUDE MOTORS
Milwaukee 16, Wisconsin

NUMBER M-344
NOVEMBER 30, 1959

KEY SWITCH WIRING

WARNING

IF STARTER KEY SWITCH IS NOT WIRED CORRECTLY MAGNETO COILS WILL EXPLODE

Too many coils are being returned to the factory as defective, when the actual cause of failure was incorrect wiring. (Fig. 1)

Ignition coils receive 100% inspection before leaving the factory so chances of receiving a defective one are very slight.

Fig. 1

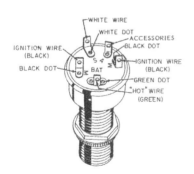

Each switch terminal has a colored dot indicating the color of the wire that should be connected to it, so if wiring must be removed for any reason be sure to <u>check</u> the <u>color code</u> before rewiring. Black wires may be interchanged on terminals marked with black dots.

The terminal marked "A" is to provide power for accessories such as lights, tachometer etc. and is live only when the key is in the "ON" position.

Figure 04-18
Magneto-equipped engines do not require a 12 volt battery in order to run; if your engine has electric start, be very careful how the starter is wired as the magneto can be damaged by 12 volt power being fed into the wrong wires.

5

Carburetors

The function of a carburetor is to supply the engine with the proper mixture of gasoline and air. It's that simple. As long as it is clean and adjusted correctly, it will function properly.

All of the hard work has already been done. Someone designed the carburetor for your engine, had the parts cast and machined, assembled and tested it and made sure that your engine would run with the thing. All you have to do is remove it from the engine, take it apart and clean it, install a few new parts, and put it back together and bolt it back onto the engine. For some reason people are often awed by carbs, but compared to fuel injection systems carbs are low-tech simple (Figure 05-01).

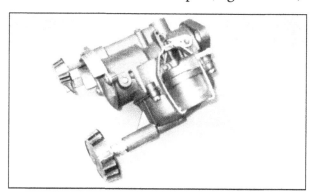

Figure 05-01
An outboard motor carburetor is basically a simple item that little can go wrong with, other than getting plugged up with debris. All you need to know is how to take it apart, clean it out, and put it back together with a few new parts.

I will suggest a good cleaning and rebuilding even if you think the carb does not need it. The rebuild kit, which should cost you less than twenty bucks, has gaskets that are resistant to the alcohol found in today's gasolines. And even if your engine runs fine as-is there may be a slug of dirt floating around in the carb just waiting to plug something up. This is usually the primary problem that carburetors will have—blocked orifices (Figure 05-02).

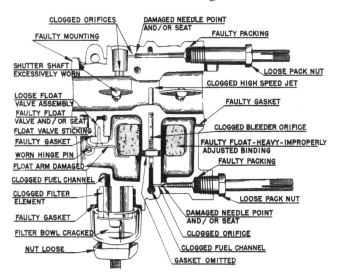

Figure 05-02
A long list of things that can go wrong with the carburetor, but notice that many of the possible faults are simply clogs.

Most of the carburetors on OMC-built outboards of up to 40 HP, and from about 1953 until about 1972, are basically very similar, differing mainly in size and in whether they are fitted with fuel/air mixture adjusting needles, or with fixed jets. In some cases, the same basic metal casting (body) is used for different size engines, the differences being in the size of internal passages and in external linkage arrangements. For this reason, the same rebuild kit will often fit several different models of

OMC outboards.

On most of the smaller engines, a choke activated by a pull-knob is used to provide a gasoline-rich fuel mixture for cold starting. On the larger motors fitted with electric start, the choke may be operated by an electric solenoid, with a pull-knob as back-up. A few 40s were even fitted with an automatic choke, but that did not work too well, and anyway a manual pull-knob was also present.

The basic design of these carbs is such that they have a portion of the carb for use at high speeds and a portion that comes into use at low speeds. The older versions of the outboards will have both high-speed and low speed mixture adjusting needles. In the early 1960s the high speed needle was replaced with a fixed "jet" which requires no adjustment, but the low speed adjusting needle remained.

One very important thing needs to be said about mixture-adjusting needle valves; they should *never* be tightened down hard on their seats. The needles are usually soft brass, and tightening down hard will usually damage the end of the needle and render proper adjustment impossible. It only takes a very slight groove on a needle to render it useless, as the metering of the fuel must be very precise, and a needle with even a slight groove on its point will not meter fuel accurately. Be very careful when tightening needle valves.

Before starting on the carb, you might want to pick up a rebuild kit. The rebuild kits from aftermarket supplier Sierra usually come with a nice set of instructions that will be of help (Figure 05-03). Carefully study these instructions before you begin.

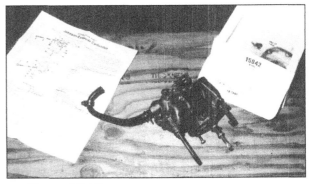
Figure 05-03
An outboard motor carburetor, a Sierra rebuild kit, and the very nice instruction sheet that comes with most Sierra carb kits.

Removing and rebuilding a carb is no big deal. The carbs on the engines in question are held on by only two nuts, but usually you must remove the cowls and recoil starter in order to gain access to the nuts. There is often an air silencer (not to be confused with an air cleaner; outboards generally do not have air cleaners) that must be removed from the carb (Figure 05-04).

Figure 05-04
The bare aluminum carburetor sits behind the white face plate and below the red intake air silencer, both of which will have to be removed before removing the carb. It is usually not necessary to remove the flywheel and magneto to get at the carb, but if you have already removed them for magneto work, hold off on reinstalling them until the carb has been removed and cleaned and reinstalled.

On some carbs it is necessary to disconnect the linkage that synchronizes the carburetor to the magneto. Usually a screw on a bell crank can be backed-off allowing the linkage to disconnect. If you are following the sequence in this book, and have left the magneto off the engine, then you can proceed to unbolting the carb from the engine by removing the nuts located on either side of the carb's mounting flange (Figure 05-05).

Figure 05-05
A wrench is hanging on one of the two mounting studs of the carburetor. Without the magneto and air silencer there isn't much to block access to the carb mountings, unless you have electric start, in which case you might have to remove the starter motor.

Once the carb has been removed you can disassemble it, usually by removing the five or six screws that hold the bowl on. With the bowl removed, the float, float needle and seat will be visible up under the upper half of the bowl. Be sure not to lose any small parts; there

are a lot of them (Figure 05-06). Keep your camera handy; a series of photos taken during disassembly may prove valuable when it comes time to put the thing back together.

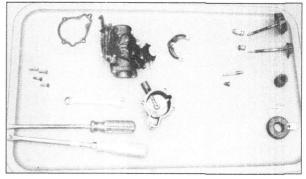

Figure 05-06
The carburetor disassembled and the necessary tools; not all that much to it, although taking good notes and a few photos would help when it comes time to put it back together, especially if you are not going to put it back together right away. Don't lose any of the parts.

Although in the past it was recommended that the carb be soaked in solvent (Figure 05-07), I have noticed that the factories have backed off on that recommendation of late, and now generally recommend using an aerosol cleaner. That is what I use.

I remove the float (usually it is varnished cork, and carb cleaner removes varnish) and needle valve, and generally a small plug on the bottom of the bowl. Most of these carbs also have a brass high-speed nozzle extending vertically up into the center of the upper half of the carb, and this too can be removed. You will notice numerous welch plugs (metal plugs, sort of like miniature auto engine "freeze plugs") that are stamped into various places on the carb body. These plugs cover the holes that were necessary in order to properly machine

Figure 05-07
The carb body halves soaking in cleaner, the old way of cleaning carbs. The old carb cleaners really did a good job, leaving you with bright, clean metal after soaking. The new "environmentally friendly" carb cleaners just do not clean as well, in my opinion. But since I mostly just use an aerosol spray now, I rarely soak carbs anymore. I keep the gallon can of cleaner around anyway; have had it for years.

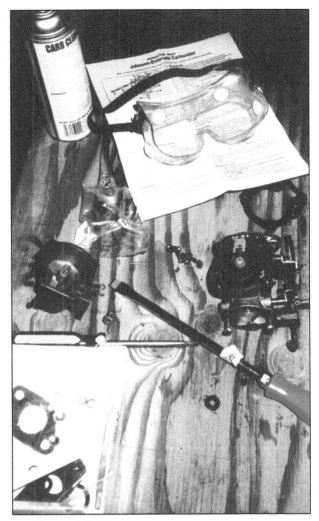

Figure 05-08
Ready to use the aerosol spray carb cleaner. The chemical protection goggles may save your eyesight. Shooting cleaner into one passage often results in the cleaner shooting out of another passage at your face. By the way, this cleaner burns bare skin. Gloves and long sleeves are advised.

the carb. Although some people recommend removing these metal plugs (which will destroy them) in order to clean underneath them, I rarely if ever disturb them. The Sierra rebuild kits that I use do contain new plugs if you really want to remove the old ones. If your carb has a fixed high-speed jet, it probably is not necessary to remove the jet itself, but you should remove the plug that covers the jet so that cleaner can be sprayed in.

Once the carb is apart, you can use the plastic tube that usually comes with the aerosol carb cleaner to shoot cleaner into all the exposed passages of the carb. Do not use wires, nails, or similar objects for cleaning carb passages, as the passages are easily damaged. Remember not to get any cleaner on the varnished cork float. If its varnish is peeling off (usually because some idiot ran automotive varnish-removing carb cleaner in the gasoline in an attempt to clean the carb while the motor was running) you might have to remove all the old loose varnish, allow the float to completely dry, and lightly sand and then re-varnish. I have used fuel-proof model airplane dope for coating cork carburetor floats.

I should point out here that you should be

wearing eye protection when spraying cleaner into passages on the carb. Many times I have shot cleaner into one hole on the carb, and had it shoot back out of another hole right at me. Safety glasses are not enough; you need chemical hazard safety goggles and probably a full face shield. Carb cleaners burn exposed skin pretty badly. It will really eat up your eyes (05-08).

Once the parts are clean and dry, you can begin reassembly. I really suggest that you use a rebuild kit when you put the carb back together, rather than just re-using the old parts. It doesn't cost that much money and may save you from having to do the job over. Keep in mind that the old "soft" parts of the carb (gaskets and such) may date from the days before alcohol (ethanol) was common in gasoline, and these parts may be harmed by exposure to alcohol.

Some things to be mindful of as the carb goes together: the float needs to be set to the proper level, so as to maintain the proper amount of gasoline in the bowl. The Sierra rebuild kits provide a nice drawing of what you are trying to achieve. The float level is adjusted by merely bending the little tap on the sheet metal hinge that the float swings on.

There is a little cork doughnut or gasket that goes over the brass high speed nozzle that some of the carbs have, extending vertically up into the upper half of the carb. Be careful when installing the doughnut that you don't tear or omit it.

Another area to be aware of is the packing which seals the mixture needle valves. Although tiny, this is basically the same sort of packing gland (stuffing box) that seals inboard propeller shafts and also valve stems. New packing is supplied in the rebuild kits. I usually just add a new ring or two of packing on top of the old stuff, since it can be hard to remove the old packing, but be careful that none ends up being pushing down into the fuel passages. The proper way to do the job is to remove all the old packing. The proper tool to use is a "packing hook," but lacking that, try an awl or an ice pick.

Once the carb is back together, you can reinstall it on the engine. Make sure the linkage to the magneto goes back together correctly, and you may need to reset the carb/mag synchronization if it was off to begin with, or if you disconnected the linkage in such a manner that it could not be put back together exactly as before. On most of these engines, synching is no big deal, being about a five-minute job needing no special tools. Usually it is just a matter of adjusting a sheet metal cam mounted on the armature plate and fitted with slotted mounting holes, until the follower (roller) of the linkage is lined up with a mark on the cam at the instant the carb butterfly begins to open (Figure 05-09).

I always replace all the fuel hoses as the old ones may be rotted and if they are not rotted, alcohol in the gas may soon rot them. Use good clamps on the hoses. I like tiny little worm-screw clamps (I think the British call them "cheney clips") when I can find them small enough. I also always install a small plastic in-line fuel filter on the engine, even if it has its original strainer/filter/sediment bowl. If I am going to spend some time and money cleaning and rebuilding a carb, I want to make

CAM FOLLOWER ADJUSTMENT
If throttle does not close, either the throttle return spring is too weak and should be replaced or the throttle or linkage is binding.

To adjust cam follower, throttle control must be advanced to the position where the cam follower roller rests on the mark in the throttle cam. See diagram at right. At this point the throttle valve should begin to open. If not loosen the hex head screws holding the cam to the armature base and push cam back towards rear of motor. Then pull cam forward until it contacts cam follower roller and just begins to open throttle valve. This takes up any slack in linkage (choke knob must be all the way in). Tighten hex head screws and recheck position of throttle valve.

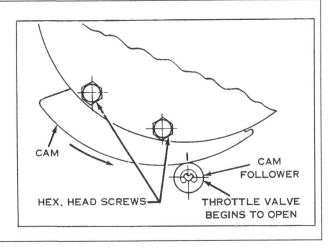

Figure 05-09: Most of the outboards under 25 horsepower use a simple roller (or even a plain metal "follower") on the carburetor linkage and a metal cam screwed to the underside of the magneto in order to sychronize the magneto spark adavance to the carburetor throttle (butterfly) valve. Larger engines sometimes used a more complicated linkage that may or may not have a "fuel saver" feature intended to reduce fuel consumption at cruising speeds.

sure that only clean fuel is running through it.

The manufacturer recommended initial mixture needle valve settings for starting an engine after the carb had been worked on, usually by giving the number of turns "open" from the fully-closed position. Lacking information on those settings, you can try setting both needles at between three-quarters of a turn open and one full turn open. After the engine is running and warmed up, final adjustments can be made to the mixture needle valve settings. This should be done with the motor on a boat, not with the motor running in a bucket of water. The normal procedure is to get the boat up on plane and to first adjust the high speed needle to give the fastest speed, then slow down and adjust the slow speed needle to give the slowest reliable idle. Make each adjustment slowly and in small increments, and allow the motor a few seconds to adjust to the new setting before making any additional adjustments. Running a bit "rich" is better than running too

"lean." A lean mixture can cause the engine to run hot and since the lubricating oil is mixed with the gasoline, starving the engine for gas also starves it for oil. When in doubt, a needle adjusted slightly rich (counter-clockwise, maybe one-sixteenth of a turn) isn't going to hurt anything.

Make sure that the packing nuts are tight enough so that vibration does not change the needle settings and air or gasoline does not leak past the packing.

6

Water Pump Repairs

Changing a water pump impeller is usually a relatively simple job that is complicated by the fact that the pump is buried deep inside the engine. Still, on most of the old OMC outboards changing an impeller is a very do-able task. The impellers used in nearly all OMC-built outboards from about 1952 until present day are all readily available through the parts sources already discussed, with some exceptions.

Before we actually begin the work, however, let's have a look at the OMC water pump situation of the late 1940s and very early 1950s. One of the reasons why I suggest you only consider engines built after about 1955 will become apparent.

The first exception is the very early Evinrude 7.5 HP that had a neutral clutch instead of a full gearshift (the engine rotated 180 degrees for reverse and there was no Johnson version of this model.) This engine used a "finned" impeller very similar to the slightly later OMC engines, but of a size that is now difficult to find. The one bright spot is that I have seen someone take an impeller from a later 1950s OMC outboard and reduce its thickness on a belt sander and was able to get the engine to pump water but I don't know

if that is a long-term solution. Better to just avoid this model. Later 7.5 HP Johnsons and Evinrudes with a full forward-neutral-reverse gearshift use a very common impeller that is easy to find.

Other exceptions are the oscillator pumps often seen on engines built by the Gale division of OMC. Instead of the usual finned impeller, the oscillator pumps used a rubber ring with a protruding nub. These rotor impellers, as I call them, were used in 5 HP Gale engines that lacked a full gearshift or a neutral clutch. However, if you have a Gale 5 with a full F-N-R gearshift, then it will use the same impeller as its contemporary Johnson and Evinrude 5.5's (Figure 06-01).

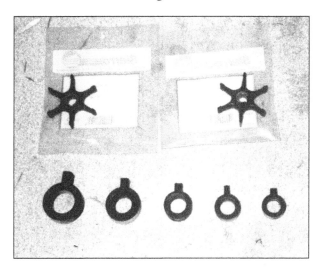

Figure 06-01　　At the top are two cooling water pump impellers of the type used on virtually all OMC outboards manufactured after about 1953, with some exceptions. The bottom row are the exceptions; starting from the left, rubber oscillator-style pump impellers for Gale 12 HP non-shift models, Gale 5 HP non-shift models, Johnson non-shift 5 HP model TD-20, Johnson 2.5 HP model HD-20, and late 1940s Gale 1.5 HP models. None of these oscillator pump engines are recommended for the cheap outboard seeker.

Gale also made a 5 HP outboard with a neutral clutch and 180-degree steering for reverse that used a finned impeller similar to, but not the same as, the impeller used on the Johnson and Evinrude 5.5's. this is another impeller that is not readily available, and another model engine to avoid.

The single-cylinder Gale 3 HP (which was completely different than the contemporary Johnson and Evinrude 3's) also uses the rotor-type pump, with one added complication. The Gale 3s built in the late 1940s used the "leg" and lower unit from the 2-cylinder 5 HP and so used the same rotor as the 5 HP. The later 3s, however, used the smaller "leg" from the discontinued 1½ HP model and so use the same rotor as the little 1½ HP. Just to add more complications, the late 1940s Johnson 5 HP model TD-20, which is a very commonly-seen old outboard (that I usually don't recommend for the "cheap power" seeker) also uses a rotor-style pump, but a different rotor than the Gale 5 HP. The Gale 5 HP, however, used the same rotor as the Scott Attwater 3½s and 4s, which had no corporate connections to OMC.

Then there was the late-1940s / early-1950s Johnson 5 HP model TN, which superceded the TD and looks very much like a TD, but which has a neutral clutch and 180-degree steering for reverse (the TD has no clutch). The TN is like the Gale 5 with neutral clutch in that it uses a finned impeller that is slightly different from what the gear-shift motors used. It may the be same impeller as the Gale 5, but that is something I have yet to confirm. The late 1940s Johnson 2½ HP model HD used a rotor-type pump, but of a different size than those

already discussed. Lastly, the big 12 HP Gale of the late 1940s / early 1950s used a large rotor in those models that lacked a gearshift, while those Gale 12s *with* the forward-neutral-reverse gearshift used the same impeller as many Johnson and Evinrude models.

By the way, all OMC engines that used the rotor-style impellers have the impellers mounted directly in front of the propeller. To remove the impeller you remove the prop and a cover plate on the back of the lower unit (2 screws).

Then there is the real "wolf in sheep's clothing"; the late 1940s Evinrude (no comparable Johnson) 3.3 HP twin-cylinder model. This baby looks just like a later Evinrude 3 HP (for which there *was* a comparable Johnson) but is a totally different engine. While the later 3 HP model uses readily-available ignition components and pump impeller, the earlier 3.3 uses an older style magneto for which parts are hard to come by, and it uses a three-legged "spider" impeller which is equally difficult to find. The 3.3 HP has a sight-glass gasoline gauge on the front of its power head-mounted gas tank, which is the easiest way to differentiate them from the 3's which have no such sight glass.

Sound complicated? You betcha! You can avoid all the hassles by sticking to Johnsons and Evinrudes built after about 1954, and Gale engines that feature a full gearshift. Impellers for those are very available and very cheap. Unlike the few years that preceded it, the era of 1955 until the early '70s produced OMC engines that changed little and were remarkably consistent.

As to changing an impeller in one of the recommended engines, all you have to do is remove the lower unit, exposing the pump housing on the top of the lower unit; remove the top of the pump housing and slide the old impeller up and off the drive shaft. Slide the new impeller down the shaft so that it is seated on its drive key; re-install the pump housing top; and reinstall the lower unit.

Of course, it could not be all that simple. First of all, for an engine with a gearshift, you have to disconnect the gearshift linkage before removing the lower unit. Most OMC-built outboards of this vintage have a small removable panel on the side of the motor "leg" which can be removed to provide access to a coupler incorporated into the gearshift linkage. You merely remove the bottom bolt from the coupler and the linkage is disconnected (Figure 06-02).

Figure 06-02   The "access door" provided on some models for disconnecting the shift linkage prior to removing the lower unit. Those models without this door require you to either remove the power head to disconnect the linkage, or the lower unit must be dropped down slightly and the linkage disconnected

Some models, however, are not fitted with this removable panel; the 5.5's and the old 7.5's, for example. With these models, you must remove the power head in order to disconnect the shift linkage at the shift-lever shaft. Not as much work as it sounds, it is still more of a hassle than just removing the access panel. You need to be careful, however, upon removing the power heads on these little engines, as there is a spring-loaded seal arrangement for the crankshaft that sits atop the drive shaft. If you carefully lift the power head straight up off the leg, the seal components will be left sitting on the drive shaft, held there by nothing more than gravity. You need to carefully remove these parts and store them so they can be reinstalled in the proper order before reinstalling the power head. (Figure 06-03)

Figure 06-03   Arrow points to the seal components sitting on top of the drive shaft of a 5.5 HP outboard that has had the power head removed. Don't lose any of these pieces and keep track of the order in which they are installed. Consider replacing the gasket that the power head sits on while you have the engine apart. The power head is removed on this model so that the linkage for the shift lever can be disconnected and the lower unit removed.

Another complication for the 5.5 and 7.5 models is that the seal components rest on a "roll pin" installed in the drive shaft, and this roll pin must be removed in order to remove the upper pump housing and the impeller from the drive shaft.

Another concern; the gaskets under the power heads of the 5.5s and the old 7.5s look very similar but are different. Using the wrong gasket will lead to overheating. I ran across this problem in an old 7.5 that I bought for twenty bucks because the previous owner could not trouble-shoot its overheating problem. It took me a while to figure that one out. If the gasket is in good condition, it can be reused. But keep in mind that a gasket that is compressed too much can reduce the end-play in the drive shaft-to-crankshaft splines. This means the crankshaft would have upward pressure against it, which increases wear and reduces power output. When the engine is all reassembled, you should be able to lift up on the flywheel and detect a very slight amount of upward movement. Of course, too much is as bad as none—we are talking about a few thousands of an inch here.

There are also a few models that do not have the access door, but that do not require the power head to be removed. Instead, you unbolt the lower unit and allow it to drop down as far as the shift shaft will allow, then the shaft coupler can be unscrewed by reaching in with a long regular head screwdriver. Some of the low-profile models (which I usually do not recommend for cheap power) are like this, as are very early 1950s Big Twins (Figure 06-04 & 06-05).

Figure 06-04
Lower unit of a 1953 25 HP model partially removed so that a regular head screwdriver can be inserted into the gap in order to remove the lower screw from the shift lever clamp, disconnecting the shift linkage and allowing the lower unit to be totally removed from the engine. Note a wrench laying in the gap; you will not have much more room than this to work with. Use a good light and a long screwdriver.

EVINRUDE SERVICE BULLETIN

Service Department
EVINRUDE MOTORS
Milwaukee 16, Wisconsin

BIG TWIN
NUMBER 25.-23
JUNE 14, 1954

SHIFT ROD CONNECTOR - BIG TWIN

Production is now using a new shift rod connector on all Big Twin and Fastwin models.

Connector is Part #376271 available now.

The new connector is adaptable to all Big Twins starting with 25012 serial 31693 and 25013 serial 23726.

All models of the Fastwin may use the same connector, starting with models 15012-15013.

The hex head screw attaches to the upper shift rod. Big Twin models without an opening in the side of the exhaust housing to reach the connector require removal of six pump housing to exhaust housing screws. This will drop the gear case about 1 inch and make the connector accessible. Work thru the opening from the rear as pictured. This will reduce the angle of approach to the lower connector screw.

EVINRUDE MOTORS

H. Dickerson   Service Promotion Mgr.

IMPORTANT: File this in your Service Bulletin Binder.

Figure 06-05
Cut-away photo shows the coupler that you need to disconnect in order to remove the lower unit from the early Big Twins and some other models.

Once the gear shift rod is disconnected (assuming the engine has a gearshift), the lower unit can be unbolted and removed. It is bad practice to carry around the lower unit by the drive shaft, if for no other reason than the drive shaft may slide out, allowing the lower unit to fall on your foot. The pump housing is usually held on by three screws (Figure 06-06). Remove the screws and slide the pump housing up and off the drive shaft.

Figure 06-06
The 1953 25 HP lower unit. As this is an early model, it does not have the water tube that conducts the cooling water from the pump up to the power head. On this model, the water flowed through passages in the castings. I think all OMCs built after 1954 use the tube instead.

Note that there should be a rubber O-ring in a groove at the top of the drive shaft; this is to help prevent water from getting into the lower main bearing of the power head. Remove the O-ring to allow the pump housing and impeller to slide off the drive shaft, but don't forget to put the O-ring back before rein-

stalling the lower unit on the engine.

Once the impeller is out of the pump, replace it with a new one. There are some people who have gotten it out, said "it doesn't look too bad" and reinstalled the same impeller. It ain't worth the hassle to try to save a few bucks, since impellers for most of the engines in question cost no more than about twelve bucks. I *always* replace the impeller in any engine that I am going to run, whether the old one is still pumping or not (Figure 06-07).

Figure 06-07
The impeller on the left is a new Sierra impeller; the impeller on the right was removed from an engine and is in bad shape. If you do not replace your impeller you risk not only ruining your day on the water, but possibly ruining your engine as well.

Before installing the impeller, however, check the housing and the metal wear plate under the impeller for wear. If they appear to be grooved, it would be best to replace them, although I have never felt the need to replace a pump housing in one of these old engines. I think I have replaced the metal plate maybe once or twice (Figure 06-08).

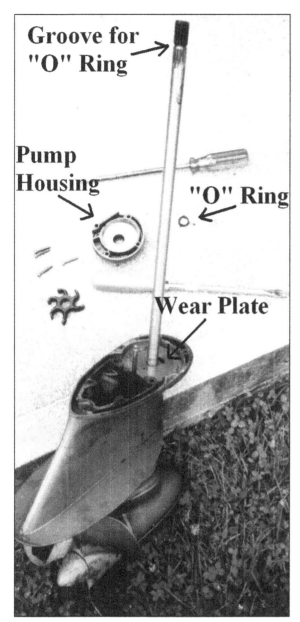

Groove for "O" Ring

Pump Housing

"O" Ring

Wear Plate

Figure 06-08
A "Big Twin" water pump disassembled and showing the various pieces including the old worn-out impeller.

Reinstalling the lower unit is usually the hardest part, as you must simultaneously align the drive shaft, shift linkage and water pump tube. Often when the lower unit is removed, the water tube will come out with the lower unit and remain attached to the pump body. Remove it from the pump body and insert it into its grommet up in the exhaust housing.

This is also a good time to inspect the water tube grommet (seal) in the pump housing. Replacing the grommet is not a bad idea.

When installing the lower unit, it helps if you can slowly rotate the flywheel to aid engagement of the crankshaft splines. The flywheel should only be rotated clockwise, the direction it rotates when the engine is running. Rotating the flywheel counter-clockwise can damage the water pump impeller.

Be sure the water tube enters the grommet on the pump housing. Connecting the shift linkage comes last—be sure the shift rod from the lower unit is fully seated in the coupler. It will take a while if you have not done this before; try to get the engine vertical and high off the ground when trying to reinstall the lower unit.

It goes without saying to be sure all bolts are snugged up tight; a little "anti-seize" compound is a good idea, especially for engines used in salt water. Make sure the engine shifts properly and also make sure cooling water is circulating before heading out on a cruise. Also have a look at the factory service bulletins in this chapter for some items to be aware of when working on the water pump.

Evinrude

Service Bulletin

Service Department
EVINRUDE MOTORS
Milwaukee 16, Wisconsin

MISCELLANEOUS
NUMBER M-214
July 8, 1957

WATER PUMP SERVICE - ALL MODELS

This bulletin supplements No. M-66, July 19, 1954.

When servicing the gearcase of any Evinrude motor, make the following inspections of the water pump to insure the owner of peak performance.

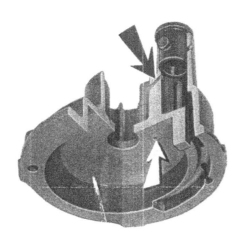

IMPELLER HOUSING PLATE - Check the impeller housing plate for flatness at the edges. If it is not true, or if doubtful, replace it.

Assemble plate with openings properly aligned and raised center area up, next to the pump impeller.

IMPELLER PIN - Inspect the impeller pin for wear. If bent or damaged, replace it.

WATER PUMP IMPELLER - Test the impeller hub to be sure a good bond exists. Failure of the bond can cause inadequate water flow at high speeds. If in doubt, or if rubber appears soft or spongy, replace the impeller.

WATER PUMP IMPELLER HOUSING - Clear openings of foreign matter - particularly the water seal supply hole (black arrow) and air escape hole (white arrow). If either of these holes become clogged, high speed pump failure may result. Pass a piece of wire through them to be sure they are open.

Check the impeller housing face for trueness. If necessary, resurface it. Use care, removing only enough stock to give a flat surface.

WATER TUBE GROMMET - Oil the water tube grommet before assembly into the housing. Oil the water tube before assembly into the grommet. This prevents the grommet from stretching and possibly closing the water seal supply hole (black arrow). Do not use grease for these operations.

EVINRUDE MOTORS

R. E. Burr

Service Promotion

R. E. Burr
smb

Figure 06-09
A few items to check while your water pump is apart.

EVINRUDE
Service Bulletin

Service Department
EVINRUDE MOTORS
Milwaukee 16, Wisconsin

TROUBLE SHOOTING
BULLETIN NO. 389
SEPTEMBER 20, 1960

OVERHEATING - CYLINDER HEAD GASKET REPLACEMENT, ALL MODELS

Always replace the cylinder head gasket on all engines that have overheated. This is extremely important, as heat will cause the gasket to dry out, shrink and lose its ability to seal combustion chambers and water passages.

Before installing the new gasket, always check the flatness of the cylinder head gasket surface on a surface plate. Heat may have caused it to warp slightly and if this is not corrected, the new gasket again will dry out and allow combustion pressures to enter the cooling system. This not only will intensify the heating problem, but in extreme cases will cause erosion across the ends of the cylinders.

Whenever overheating problems are encountered on any engine, the normal recommended procedure is to check out the following possible causes:

1. An inoperative water pump due to faulty or worn pump parts, such as:
   (a) Impellers
   (b) Housings
   (c) Pump Plates
   (d) Grommets
   (e) Seals
2. Clogged or obstructed water passages, hoses, intake screens, etc. due to:
   (a) Corrosion - particularly in salt water areas.
   (b) Metal flashing, a thin film of metal, left in as a result of die casting.
   (c) Other foreign matter or objects.
3. Clogged water jackets and passages in cylinder blocks and heads. Look for the same causes as listed under No. 2, a, b, and c preceding.
4. Inoperative thermostats, vernatherms, or water pressure valves on all engines equipped with thermostatically controlled cooling systems.
5. Faulty gaskets and water hose connections.

After making certain that the cause of overheating has definitely been corrected, replace ALL affected cooling system gaskets and as your final corrective action always replace the cylinder head gasket as outlined above.

EVINRUDE MOTORS

Richard Bayley

Service Promotion

Figure 06-10
Considering the difficulty in locating new cylinder head gaskets for some of the older OMC engines, along with the possibility of breaking head bolts, I generally ignore the factory's advice to always replace the cylinder head gasket on an engine which has overheated, unless there is an obvious problem with the gasket. Good trouble-shooting suggestions.

EVINRUDE
SERVICE BULLETIN

Service Department
EVINRUDE MOTORS
Milwaukee 16, Wisconsin

MISCELLANEOUS
NUMBER M-66
JULY 19, 1954

PUMP HOUSING ALL MODELS

This bulletin is a summary on the complete function of current pump housing.

The figure on the left is explanatory of the housings on the Lightwin, Fleetwin and Fastwin. You will note the position of the water tube grommet and its relation to the water passage (black arrows) from the pressure (or outlet) side of the pump into the well in the top of the housing. This passage supplies water to the drive shaft entry into the pump housing for sealing exhaust gas from entering the pump.

The water well must be filled at all times while the motor is running, otherwise the pump may fail during high speed motor operation.

The water tube grommet must be oiled as well as the water tube at the time of assembly. Failure to lubricate these parts may cause the water tube to stretch the grommet across the water passage, (black arrow) and close the passage. It is advisable to remove burrs and sharp edges from the water tube before it enters the grommet.

Continuing with the left view you will note a white arrow pointing to a small drilled hole that also enters the well on top of the pump housing. This hole eliminates air locking within the pump and also contributes water to the well above for sealing purposes.

Should either one of the water entries to the well (passage or drilled hole) be restricted or closed the pumping action at high speeds will be questionable.

In the right view (Big Twin) the white arrow has exactly the same duty as described above. The black arrow also indicating the water passage to the well. The water tube grommet is located in the exhaust housing and will therefore not interfere or close the water passage to the well. It's essential to oil this grommet as well as the water tube before assembly to avoid cutting or tearing the grommet, creating a pressure leak.

Oil is recommended as a lubricant for the grommets and water tube rather than grease. In the left view it can be readily seen that excess grease could easily fill and block the water passage to the water well.

EVINRUDE MOTORS

Figure 06-11
The drive shaft opening in the pump housing is sealed with water rather than a mechanical seal, and if the water seal's passages are plugged, exhaust gas can get into the pump and destroy its ability to pump water.

Evinrude
Service Bulletin

Service Department
EVINRUDE MOTORS
Milwaukee 16, Wisconsin

MISCELLANEOUS
NUMBER M 168
DATE 4-18-56

WATER INTAKE SYSTEM

Water entering the motor for cooling purposes will be taken in at one position when operating with the regular propeller and a different location when operating with a test propeller. The bypass cover is shown removed to expose the water passage.

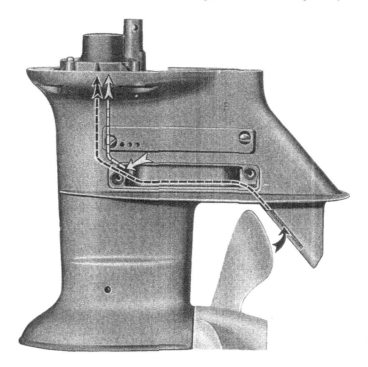

During normal boat operation, the bypass cover is to be attached with the holes in the cover facing forward. Water will enter at the point indicated by the black arrow and follow the path shown to the water pump. The wash from the propeller blades and the forward motion of the lower unit through the water assist in directing water to the pump. After the water reaches the pump, it is forced through the cooling system under positive pressure.

When operating a motor in a test tank, the bypass cover should be removed and a test propeller used. The test propeller does not provide wash to the normal water intake point nor is the lower unit moving forward to benefit from scooping action. Therefore, water enters at the point shown by the white arrow and has only a short travel to reach the water pump.

NOTE: Make sure the bypass cover is in place before the motor is used on the water.

It is essential that a test propeller be used on a motor undergoing test tank analysis.

See Bulletin ▓▓▓▓▓ for complete data on the various test propellers.
M-166

EVINRUDE MOTORS

Figure 06-12

I have encountered an engine or two with the exhaust bypass passages plugged with crud; something else to check when trouble-shooting an overheating engine. Also note that an outboard motor can easily overheat while being run in a test tank (your garbage can?).

Service Department
EVINRUDE MOTORS
Milwaukee 16, Wisconsin

MISCELLANEOUS
NUMBER M-286
September 29, 1958

WATER PUMP IMPELLERS

Investigation of numerous water pump impeller failures has revealed that motors are being run out of water for one reason or another, including draining the carburetor of fuel and draining the motor of water.

This is a dangerous practice and should not be done under any circumstances. Among other results of running a motor out of water is the fact that the rubber impeller will not hold up running in a dry pump. The blades will scuff, get hot, and break.

Also, if it is necessary to turn over the motor by hand during repair be certain it is turned over in its normal direction of movement. Turning in reverse direction may also result in impeller damage.

EVINRUDE MOTORS

William B. Smale
Service Promotion

Figure 06-13
Do not run a water-cooled outboard unless water is being supplied to it by either submerging the lower unit in a test tank or through the use of a flush attachment. Even a few seconds of running is enough to ruin the impeller.

7

Recoil Starters

Don't ya just love it. It's cold and raining and you're out on the water in an open boat. A big, soft, cushy, couch and hot drink are just a few minutes motor'n away. You grab the starter rope on your trusty ole' outboard and give it a yank. As you pull back, the rope separates from the pull-handle and you watch the rope slither back into the motor to disappear, leaving you with the starter handle in your hand and a forty-five-minute row back to the hot drink.

Major bummer.

Actually, since your outboard is an old OMC, you can always remove the cowl and recoil starter, and wrap any handy piece of rope around the emergency starter sheave (which most 1950s Mercurys don't have) and get your prime mover started. But then, if you had regularly inspected your engine's starter rope, and replaced it when it began to look questionable, the above scenario probably would not have happened.

Not only is the above incident a pain to deal with, there is a good chance that the recoil starter, rewinding violently when it was released from its load, has kinked the recoil starter spring, ruining it.

The recoil starters we will be discussing here are those which sit on top of OMC-manufactured engines from the mid 1950s until the early '70s. A few OMCs of this period, notably the 6 HP and the 9½, use a side-mounted starter that engages a flywheel ring gear. These buggers are a much bigger problem to deal with and we will not address them here (Figure 07-01).

Figure 07-01
The light-colored recoil starter is mounted atop the power head by three screws and is easily removed once the cowl (hood) is removed.

From the mid-1950s to the early 1970s, there were mainly two different types of "top-mounted" starters used on OMCs; the "simplex" (Figure 07-02) and the "eas-a-matic." (Figure 07-03). They are actually very similar, the main difference being that the simplex uses three spring-loaded metal pawls to engage the top of the flywheel, while the "eas-a-matic" uses a single plastic pawl to engage the flywheel. The simplex also has a few extra parts to

Figure 07-02
A "simplex" starter; note the three "arms" for engaging the flywheel. Also note that this older-model simplex is actually mounted to the cowling of the engine whereas the starter in figure 07-01 is mounted to the power head.

Figure 07-03
The underside of an "ease-a-matic" starter. Note the oblong shape of the sheave upon which the rope winds. If the starter is timed correctly, the shape of the sheave provides for easier starting.

it. Replacing ropes or springs is about the same for either of these, however.

Replacing a starter rope is usually no big deal. Remove the recoil starter from the engine and turn it upside down. You will see, on the rope sheave, the knot where the "bitter end" of the rope is secured. If the rope is really old, it may have a metal fitting on the end, and the rope itself may be a natural fiber surrounding a metal cable core.

Regardless of what is already in there, I always replace my starter ropes with braided nylon from the hardware store. It is probably not the ideal rope for the job, but is cheap and easy to find. Try to get some that matches the diameter of the existing rope. About the most you will need will be seven feet. Figure 07-04 is an old OMC service bulletin listing the diameters and lengths for the starter ropes of some pre-1962 engines. Always check the length of the old rope before cutting the new one, but keep in mind that the existing rope in the engine may have been an improper replacement installed some time in the past. I would add a few inches to the recommended lengths, just in case. It is easy to shorten a rope, but rather difficult to lengthen one.

The end of the rope is secured into the "pull handle" by threading the rope through a metal retainer, which can be pried out of the end of the rubber handle (07-05). If your pull handle is damaged or missing, there is no reason it can not be replaced with a standard lawn mower replacement from the local hardware store.

To replace the rope, pull it all the way out of the recoil starter (which you have removed from the engine, remember?) and then figure a

Johnson MOTORS

W A U K E G A N ,   I L L I N O I S

August 25, 1961

Service Bulletin

Bulletin No. SB-864
Manual Starters

DEALER	✓
SERVICE MGR.	
SALES MGR.	
PARTS MGR.	
SERVICE MGR.	

SUBJECT: Change in servicing nylon starter ropes;
All engine models from 1956 thru current & future models.

As soon as distributors' stocks of current starter ropes are exhausted, only two basic ropes will be serviced. These two ropes are part numbers 204085 (7/32" diameter) and 203819 (5/32" diameter), from which all starter ropes for the various engine models must be made by cutting them to the required length specified in the following table.

35 hp (2-piece hood)
10 hp
15 hp
18 hp
30 hp
50 hp
35 hp (one-piece hood)

7/32" Diameter Ropes		5/32" Diameter Ropes	
TO MAKE ROPE NO.	CUT #204085 to LENGTH SHOWN	TO MAKE ROPE NO.	CUT #203819 TO LENGTH SHOWN
204085	75 3/4" (Basic rope)	203819	71½" (Basic Rope) —— 5 1/2 hp
203821	72 1/4"	203817	68 5/16" —— 3 hp
203822	70 3/16"	203818	66 3/4"
304096	69 3/4"	203820	70"
305000	73 3/4"	304097	63 3/4"

(Engines newer than 1962 may differ from above lengths)

After the rope has been cut to the correct length, the cut end must be singed to prevent fraying by gently applying heat around the circumference with a lighter or match.

The timing of the starter is affected by the placement of the knot at the end of the rope as well as by the rope's length. When the rope is cut to the required length shown and the know is placed 1/2" from the end (1/2" of rope protruding from knot), the starter is correctly timed. This can be checked by aligning the correct timing marks.

If for some reason the cutting length of a given rope is not available, proceed as follows:
Install the rope as usual to the point of having the handle on the rope. Let the starter rewind until the timing marks are in alignment and put a knot in the rope so it won't pull through the handle. Allow enough rope to thread the anchor; then cut to the required length, singe the cut end, remove the knot, and thread the anchor. The timing should be correct when the anchor is placed in the handle.

Past parts catalogs specify one of the old rope numbers for a given engine model. To determine which of the two (2) basic ropes to use when replacing a starter rope, refer to the appropriate parts catalog for the engine being serviced, and note the rope number specified. Then refer to the table contained in this bulletin to determine which basic rope to use and the length to which it must be cut.

The 1962 Master Parts Price list will also contain the table shown in this bulletin. After these price lists are received by you, reference should be made to it to determine the basic rope to use and the proper length to which it must be cut.

Future parts catalogs, instead of specifying the old rope numbers, will specify one of the two (2) basic rope numbers along with the correct length.

JOHNSON MOTORS

W. W. DeWees,

W. W. DeWees
Service Department

WWD:eb
NOTE: Post on all indexes, JW thru V-75

Figure 07-04   The length of the starter rope directly affects the timing of the eas-a-matic starters. Also note that two different diameter starter ropes where used in the engines. As the older simplex starters where not timed, starter rope length is not so critical to easy starting.

Figure 07-05
The metal retainers which secure the starter ropes to the pull handles. Note that there are two different diameter starter ropes and thus two different retainers. There is only one size of rubber handle.

way to hold the rope sheave from re-winding. Sometimes some of these sheaves have a hole through them where you can insert a special pin (nail) to lock the sheave to the housing. Or you can use a pair of locking pliers (Vise Grips) to lock the sheave, but be careful not to cause damage. Usually, I just hold the sheave and housing with one hand so as to lock them together, and then remove the old rope by cutting-off the retaining knot.

Insert the new rope though the guide hole of the housing and into the sheave and through the knot hole. I usually use a figure-eight knot to secure the end of the rope. You can then let the sheave wind the rope back in, but if you have not attached the handle to the other end, don't let the recoil suck the rope all the way in. Make sure your knot is not so massive that the flywheel rubs it.

On the eas-a-matic starters you will notice that the sheave that the rope is wrapped on is oval-shaped instead of round. Some engineering minds in the OMC design department fig-

ured out that a person needed more leverage on the starter rope during the compression stroke, and could use the non-compression portion of the stroke to build up speed in the rotation. The oval-shaped sheave accomplishes this, but only if it is properly aligned in respect to the crankshaft. These starters will have a small arrow cast into the housing. This arrow should align with marks on the rope sheave when the starter is at rest. If it does not, adjust the length of the rope at the handle until it does. This is referred to as "timing" the starter and getting it right will make your outboard a bit easier to start (Figure 07-06). If you have cut your new rope a bit longer than recommended, you can fine-tune the timing of the starter by cutting off the end as needed.

If you are installing a rope in a starter where the sheave has been allowed to unwind and is no longer under tension, you will need to "pre-load" the spring when installing the new rope. Coil up your rope on top of the sheave in order to determine how many rotations of the sheave are needed in order to "pre-load" the spring so it will pull the rope all the way back and not leave it hanging (07-07). If you have too much "pre-load" you risk breaking the spring plus you are making additional work for whoever has to start the motor. Once you have pre-loaded the spring by rotating the sheave in the direction of engine rotation, you are ready to install the rope as previously discussed.

A bigger job than replacing the starter rope is replacing the spring. The spring in the top-mounted recoil starters is about a 6-foot-long strip of spring steel, coiled up between the

Evinrude
Service Bulletin

Service Department
EVINRUDE MOTORS
Milwaukee 16, Wisconsin

MISCELLANEOUS
NUMBER M-144
September 30, 1955

EAS-A-MATIC STARTER TIMING

Starter rope length is the key to timing the starter.

Note the arrow and the box identified by E. The arrow should point inside the limit marks when the starter is properly timed.

Pictured is a new starter that is assembled but never operated. The arrow is just outside the limit and this is because the rope has never been pulled. As soon as the starter is placed on a motor and operated 5 or 6 pulls the rope will stretch slightly and the arrow will then indicate within limits.

Each starter for 1956 will have a proper rope size and length noted by color on the ends of the rope. The 1956 Big Twin uses a Simplex starter and is therefore excluded from the above information. The 1955 Big Twin rope is the same as one used in the 1956 model.

Use only the 1956 rope anchors and handles on the EAS-A-MATIC starters.

EVINRUDE MOTORS

Figure 07-06
The purpose of eas-a-matic starter timing is to provide extra leverage on the compression stroke.

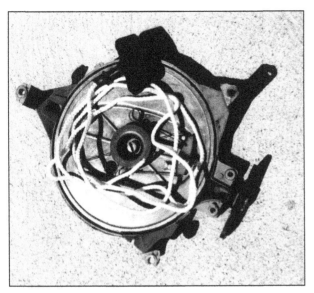

Figure 07-07
Coiling the correct length of starter rope on top of the sheave to count the number of turns necessary to pre-load the spring.

housing and the rope sheave, and just waiting to jump out at you. It is very important to wear eye protection when attempting spring replacement, and a full face shield would not be a bad idea. So would gloves, but I can't seem to work in gloves so I don't use them (Figure 07-08).

Figure 07-08
Before you start to disassemble one of these starters, be sure that you have eye protection. The goggles are good, but a full face shield is better.

The tension must be removed from the spring before the spring can be removed. If the rope broke, that has already been taken care of; if not, you can cut the rope or remove the handle from the rope and allow the sheave to unwind completely.

One large screw in the center of the sheave holds the whole thing together. Remove that screw and you can remove the sheave from the housing *but* be aware that the spring is still a threat, even if it has been allowed to unwind (Figure 07-09).

The spring is held within a circular recess in the housing, and the spring will unwind to the point that it rests against the recess. If the spring comes out of that recess, it will unwind more, and very rapidly, if it is uncontrolled. One end of the spring has an "eye" which is sitting on a pin mounted to the housing. The other end of the spring has an eye which engages a pin mounted to the sheave. You have

Figure 07-09
Using an impact driver to loosen the center screw of the recoil starter. These impact drivers use a hammer and only cost about $15.00 or so for a cheap one.

to very carefully remove the sheave without allowing its pin to drag the spring out of its recess, because once the spring starts to come out, it's coming out and you had better stay out of the way.

Keep your face and exposed skin clear as you carefully remove the sheave. This will reveal the spring sitting in its recess (Figure 07-10).

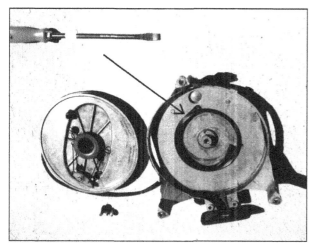

Figure 07-10
Once the driver has loosened the center screw, an ordinary screwdriver can be used to remove the screw and the sheave can be carefully lifted out of the housing. Arrow points to the spring coiled up in its recess. If the spring "hangs up" on the sheave as you remove the sheave, the spring will come whipping out of the housing.

At this point you can either carefully remove the spring by hand, keeping a tight grip on it or you can just toss the housing onto the ground and the spring will remove itself pronto. Be sure to toss it several feet away from you and it would be easier on the starter if you toss it into grass rather than onto concrete.

The recoil starter in the photos was still operating when the decision was made to replace the spring. But note that the old spring

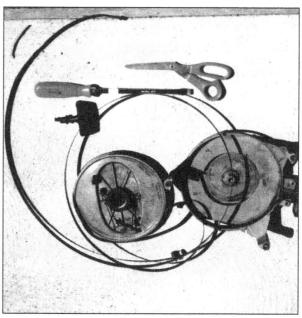

Figure 07-11
The old spring out of the housing. It retains a coiled shape. A new spring will be almost straight. The scissors were used to cut the handle off the old starter rope and the starter allowed to unwind at a controlled rate.

maintains some of its coil shape, indicating that it has seen better days (Figure 07-11). A new spring will be straight when at rest.

I will now explain how I install the new spring. This is how I do it and is not necessarily how others do it nor the factory recommended it be done. OMC had special tools which could be used to easily accomplish the job; I have a few of the tools but never use them. I will suggest that you first try reassembling the starter without the spring in order to become thoroughly familiar with how the parts fit together. After a successful dry-run, you are then ready for the real thing. Disassemble the starter but have all the parts within easy reach.

Starting with a stretched-out new spring, I place the outer eye (eye without a bend in the

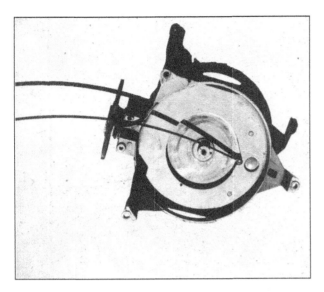

Figure 07-12
The eye for the "housing end" of the new spring has been placed on its pin in the housing, and the spring can now be carefully wrapped into its recess.

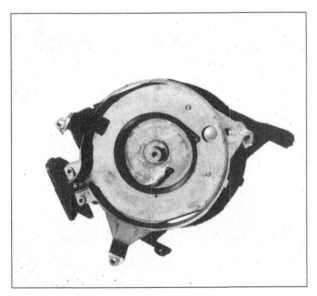

Figure 07-13
The spring has been wrapped into its recess. ANY JARRING MOVEMENT MAY CAUSE THE SPRING TO COME LOOSE—USE EXTREME CAUTION!!

spring next to it) on its pin on the housing and slowly coil the spring into the recess in the housing (Figure 07-12). This is a bit tedious, as it is easy to lose control and have the spring come back out of the recess in a hurry. It takes

patience and a bit of manual dexterity, and keep the kids away. BE SURE TO WEAR EYE AND FACE PROTECTION!

Once you have successfully coiled the entire spring into the recess, don't breathe a sign of relief. The hard part is still to come (Figure 07-13). Keep in mind all the time that you cannot allow the spring to start to come out of that recess as it will keep coming! The trick is to install the sheave back in the housing and engage the pin on the sheave with the eye on the inner end of the spring (Figure 07-14).

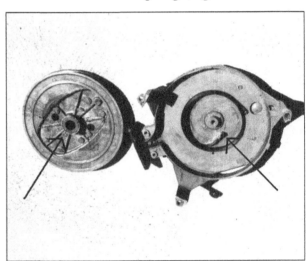

Figure 07-14
Left arrow points to the pin on the sheave which must engage the inner eye on the spring (right arrow). Note that the sheave is pictured upside-down and must be flipped to install in the housing.

What I usually do is take a pair of pliers and give the end of the spring a slight twist, before I start to wrap it into the housing, so that the eye stands slightly proud from the surface of the recess. With the eye slightly high, you can first engage the pin, and then concentrate on getting the sheave on. If you put too much twist on the spring, it will not stay in the recess. This is tedious work and it will probably take you several tries; be patient, be careful, and don't allow your frustrations to rule your actions. If necessary, walk away from the thing for a while. If you get into a hurry or allow your frustrations to take over, you risk injury to yourself or the starter. Take your time, study the pieces, and resign yourself to spending a bit of time on your first one.

And *always* be mindful of that spring!

There is another way to do this without special tools, although I prefer not to it do this way. Many of the rope sheaves have a hole in them which can be lined up with the pin mounted on the housing. The method here is to install the inner eye of the spring on the sheave and wrap the spring up on the sheave and secure the outer eye of the spring with a pin inserted through the hole in the sheave. The sheave is then placed into the housing, taking care to line up your temporary pin with the housing pin, and as the sheave is pushed down into the housing, the outer eye will be pushed down onto the housing pin, and the housing pin will push out your temporary pin. I don't like the idea of trying to transfer the eye of a spring under tension from one pin to another, so I do not use this method, but it might work for you.

With either method, once the sheave is down in the housing and the center screw installed, the hard part is done and you can now install the rope as detailed at the beginning of this chapter.

The recoil starters we are talking about here are not high-tech rocket science; they are simple mechanical devices consisting of only four main parts; housing, rope sheave, rope and spring.

One final comment about these recoil starters: occasionally I have run across a starter that would rewind itself very slowly while making a noise like a swarm of hornets. This can often be caused by excessive wear to the internal components. Often this wear can be compensated for by removing a bit of material from the spindle, as detailed in Figure 07-15, eliminating the noise and improving the operation of the starter.

Evinrude
Service Bulletin

Service Department
EVINRUDE MOTORS
Milwaukee 16, Wisconsin

MISCELLANEOUS
NUMBER M-176
July 16, 1956

STARTER SPINDLE REPAIR

After considerable use, a starter spindle may wear and become noisy. A simple correction will eliminate end play and restore the starter to quiet operation.

The spindle shown left is from an Eas-A-Matic Starter while the one on the right is from a Simplex Starter. In either case, removing a few thousandths of an inch from the upper surface of the spindle (see arrows) will reduce end play in the rope pulley and eliminate the noise.

Proceed by placing a sheet of emery cloth on a flat surface and dress the upper surface of the spindle. Rotate the spindle between strokes to equalize the removal of stock.

Reduce the end play to a minimum but do not remove it entirely as a slight amount of end play is required.

In the case of the Simplex spindle, it is necessary to remove the small locating pin prior to the dressing operation.

Part #203699   Eas-A-Matic starter spindle

Part #276643   Simplex Starter Spindle

EVINRUDE MOTORS

H Dickerson

Service Promotion Mgr.

Figure 07-15
A noise resembling a swarm of angry hornets may be caused by excessive wear, and can sometimes be corrected by removing a small amount of material from the spindle. Note the differences between simplex and eas-a-matic spindles.

8

Fuel Tanks

~

There are basically two types of fuel tanks used on outboard motors; the smallest engines generally use tanks mounted on the power head and feed gasoline to the engine via gravity. There is little to go wrong with this system, short of a clogged tank vent or plugged fuel filter (Figure 08-01). The 3 HP Johnson and Evinrude used this style of fuel tank, although in the late 1960s a kit was available to convert the late 3HP models to use a fuel pump and remote tank. These conversions are rarely seen, though.

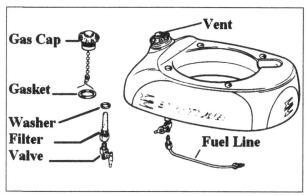

Figure 08-01

A power head-mounted, gravity-fed fuel tank such as fitted to the 3 HP models.

Almost all outboards but the very smallest will utilize a remote tank; i.e., a tank sitting somewhere in the boat with a rubber fuel line that leads to the engine. All modern outboards, and many old ones, are fitted with a

fuel pump that draws the fuel through the hose and up to the engine. Usually the fuel hose is fitted with a squeeze-bulb for manually pumping fuel to the engine for starting. As with the power head-mounted tanks, there is not too much that can go wrong with one of these tanks, so we will not spend much time on them. Just keep in mind that the two biggest problems that occur with this type of tank is a plugged filter on the fuel pick-up tube inside the tank, or a vacuum leak which will most likely be caused by the fuel hose rather than the tank itself. The hose can have a leak as can the rubber primer bulb, or a quick connector can have a bad O-ring seal. The fuel pump mounted on the engine sucks fuel from the tank through the hose, and if there is a leak somewhere, the pump will suck air instead of fuel. A common cause of these vacuum leaks is a connector that is not fully seated into position. If you suspect a problem, the first thing to check is that the connectors are truly connected.

A typical OMC factory tank is shown in Figures 08-02 and 08-03: tanks made by other manufacturers will be similar. After about 1960, all OMC built outboard motors that used remote fuel tanks were fitted with fuel pumps and used this style tank. In addition, some earlier outboards, particularly the Gale versions, also used this style of tank. If your fuel pump-style-engine did not come with a tank, or if the tank is rusted or extremely dirty, a new plastic fuel tank may be purchased from either a boat dealer or from a discount store. Pick up a new fuel hose at the same time and be sure that the hose has the proper fittings to fit both your engine and also the tank as some

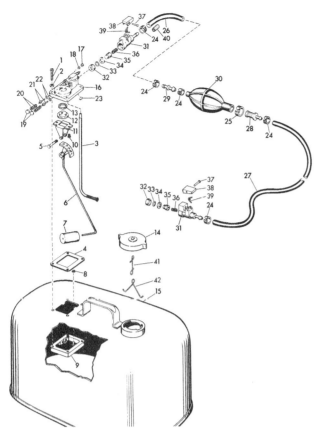

Figure 08-02 and 08-03 (parts index)
Diagram of an OMC factory remote fuel tank intended for outboard motors fitted with fuel pumps. Aftermarket "generic" tanks will be similar.

tanks use a quick connector to attach the hose to the tank and other tanks have the fuel hose permanently clamped to the tank. Either will work fine; just a matter of personal preference.

A pressure tank is a remote tank as well, but the engine does not use a fuel pump to draw fuel through the hose. Instead, the tank is pressurized though one passage in a two-passage hose, and the gasoline is forced by this pressure back up the other passage in the hose to the engine. These tanks operate at a pressure of about 2 to 3 PSI. (Figure 08-04).

Operating an outboard that uses a pressure tank is only slightly different from operating an outboard with the fuel-pump-style tank.

With the fuel pump motors, the primer bulb on the fuel hose is squeezed to prime the engine with fuel; the pressure tank has a built-in primer pump on the top of the tank. Because the pressure tank is, of course, under pressure, there is no vent on the tank. If you remove the lid in order to check the fuel level, you will release all the pressure and your engine will stop. I would recommend loosening the gas cap slightly to release the pressure in the tank whenever the engine is going to be shut down for more than a few minutes, so that pressure in the tank is not trying to force gasoline into the engine. Just remember to tighten the cap before starting the engine, oth-

Figure 08-04
An OMC "pressure" remote tank intended for use with outboards not fitted with fuel pumps; this is a pre-1957 tank as the primer pump has the aluminum button pinned to a shaft (see text).

erwise the engine will start and run for a moment until the gasoline in the carburetor is used up, then it will stall. The primer pump on the tank allows you to manually pump fuel into the engine for starting, and then once started, the engine quickly pressurizes the tank; the primer pump itself does not pressurize the tank. Should something go wrong with the tank, you can motor back home by constantly pumping fuel to the engine with the primer pump, at least until either the pump diaphragm or your thumb gives up.

The first OMC-built outboard to use the remote pressure tank was the 1949 Johnson 10 HP. The last to use the pressure tank was probably the 1960 5½ HP. In between, virtually every Johnson and Evinrude outboard over 3 HP used the pressure remote tank; the exceptions were a very early Evinrude 7.5 HP that

had a neutral clutch instead of a full gearshift, some 1959 models (it took two years to complete the change-over from pressure tanks to fuel pumps), and some models that were fitted with optional fuel pumps (OMC did offer conversion kits).

The first pressure tanks are referred to as "high boys" because they were relatively tall. After a few years, the "low" tanks were introduced in 4- and 6-gallon capacities, and these low tanks look fairly similar to outboard tanks used for fuel-pump engines. Oddly enough, the Gale division of OMC, which sold engines that were supposed to be "economy" models, had fuel pumps standard on their remote-tank models as far back as 1955.

So how do you identify a pressure tank? The pressure tank will always have attachments for two hoses, usually hose barbs, with one labeled FUEL and one labeled AIR. Also, an OMC pressure tank generally will have a large, removable "tank top," usually painted black, whereas most "fuel pump" tanks have a relatively small fuel-pickup assembly mounted on the top of the tank. But remember those Gale engines that came with fuel pumps back in the mid-50s? Often there were sold with remote tanks that looked very much like pressure tanks, with the large removable tank-top, but with only one hose barb outlet on top. Although you rarely see these old Gale fuel-pump tanks anymore, they are still out there, waiting to trap the unwary. Always look for the two hose connections on the top of the tank, but do not be confused by quick connectors on "fuel-pump" style tanks; these have a single hollow fuel-conducting pin with check

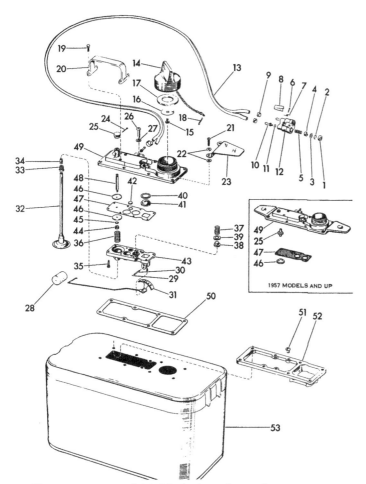

Figure 08-05 and 08-06 (index of parts) Diagram of a typical OMC pressure tank; note differences in the primer pumps between early and later tanks. Pressure tanks came in 4-gallon and 6-gallon sizes, but the mechanical "guts" are the same in both tanks.

valve on the tank connection, along with a "locking" pin which holds the connector securely in place. Pressure tanks always had the hose clamped to the gas tank; the hose was not attached to the tank with a quick connector on any pressure tank. If you frequent outboard motor swap meets, you may occasional run across a pressure tank for a Mercury outboard. Mercury switched to fuel pumps well before OMC did, and a Mercury pressure tank is a rare and valuable item. Although an old OMC outboard can be made to run with a Mercury

pressure tank, I would suggest trading a good Mercury tank for two OMC pressure tanks (Figure 08-07).

You will want to make sure that your pressure tank is complete. The caps for these pressure tanks are something special. If your tank is missing the cap, it might be difficult to replace. Another very difficult piece to replace is the quick connector that attaches the hose to the outboard. If you do not get this connector with the tank, you will have a hard time finding one for any kind of reasonable price.

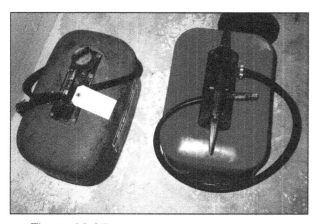

Figure 08-07
Left tank is an OMC pressure tank while on the right is a Mercury pressure tank. The Mercury tank is much harder to find and worth a lot more than the more common OMC pressure tank, another reason I advise cheap outboard seekers to avoid old Mercurys.

Several years ago when I was desperate for one, I paid $20.00 for a used one fitted with new O-rings (Figure 02-17); lately I have seen prices as high as $60.00 quoted for these things. Just for a fuel-line connector. I have seen prices of over $100.00 quoted for a useable pressure tank, hose, and fitting. Which is why you should think hard before buying an 1950s OMC outboard that needs a pressure tank but does not have one, unless you are willing to convert the outboard to use a fuel pump (see Chapter 12).

Of course, once you have your tank, what if it doesn't work? Well, if gas leaks out of the tank top when you push on the primer-pump button, chances are you have a bad primer pump diaphragm. These are sometimes available through Johnson/Evinrude dealers if you can find a parts man that is willing to look. Note that here are two different styles of primer buttons seen on these tanks; with tanks made prior to 1957 the button is an aluminum piece that is "pinned" to its shaft. On tanks made in 1957 and later, the primer button is a black, one-piece affair. It is important to correctly identify which style primer button you have because there are two different pump diaphragms used (Figure 08-08).

It is also important to install the diaphragm with the correct side "up." Also note that very early tanks differed somewhat in the valve arrangements of the diaphragm pump (08-09).

If you pump and pump and no gas comes out of the FUEL hose barb on the tank top (remove the fuel hose), there is a good chance that you have a stuck lower check valve (Figure 08-10). The primer pump is a simple diaphragm pump, with a check valve up in the tank top on the discharge side of the pump, and a check valve down inside the strainer on the bottom of the fuel pick-up tube on the suction side of the pump. Often the check valve down there at the bottom of the tube will stick due to old gasoline sitting in the tank. Take something like an awl or an ice pick and gently insert it through the strainer mesh on the bottom of the fuel pickup and push the check-valve disc loose- it should rattle when the pick-up tube is shaken. Then soak the bottom of the tube in cleaning solvent.

If there is fuel leaking out around the quick-connector where it attaches to the engine, the little O-ring seals in it can be changed. This is a tedious job that can be accomplished with a couple of simple tools made from stiff paper clips (Figure 08-11).

The O-rings are available from Johnson and Evinrude dealers and also from after market

Service Department
EVINRUDE MOTORS
Milwaukee 16, Wisconsin

MISCELLANEOUS
NUMBER M-194
December 13, 1956

PUSH BUTTON - CRUIS-A-DAY FUEL TANKS

The new Cruis-A-Day Fuel Tanks, four and six gallon sizes, features a new housing, push button and diaphragm assembly. The housing accomodates: a plastic push button, which will eliminate corrosion problems which sometimes occurred with the metal button, a new diaphragm assembly which will eliminate the leakage of fuel around the primer pump push button. The diaphragm and support plates are now riveted together making a permanent and much tighter assembly.

The priming operation will be the same except the push button will ride the top support plate (arrow) but will not be connected to it as shown below.

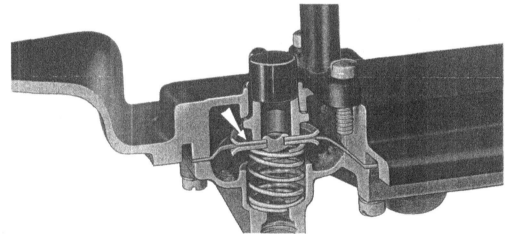

Cruis-A-Days with this new assembly can be readily identified by a large cast letter "A" on the upper housing near the push button.

Service on the present tank components will continue with one exception: The fuel tank housing - upper #376276 will be superseded by - housing, push button and diaphragm assembly #376988, when present stock is depleted. At that time the new assembly will be shipped, featuring the new push button and diaphragm, when the old housing - upper is ordered.

Order your extra new Cruis-A-Day Tanks and service parts directly from your Parts Distributor.

Figure 08-08
A cut-away illustration of the new style primer pump. "Cruis-A-Day" was the name that Evinrude applied to their pressure remote tanks; Johnson labeled theirs, "Mile-Master."

EVINRUDE
SERVICE BULLETIN

Service Department
EVINRUDE MOTORS
Milwaukee 16, Wisconsin

MISCELLANEOUS
NUMBER M-89
November 22, 1954

DIAPHRAGM, CRUIS-A-DAY TANKS

In order to explain a recent change in the diaphragm in Cruis-A-Day tanks, we will include key information to cover all installations.

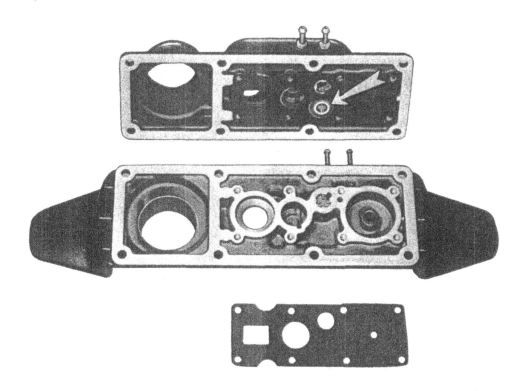

The top view shows an early type tank housing (upper) with the required diaphragm in place. The white arrow points to a pressure relief opening which was controlled by a rubber valve in the lower housing. All upper housings designed with the relief valve can use the new diaphragm shown in the lower view. This application will eliminate the relief valve function but the valve must still be used to back up the new diaphragm at that point, otherwise the diaphragm will soon rupture and fail.

NOTE: If the diaphragm shown in the top view is turned over causing the large hole (white arrow) to cover the hole directly above, the tank will fail to retain pressure.

The center view shows the latest tank housing (upper). Note the absence of the pressure relief hole. This installation requires the new diaphragm and does not require the rubber relief valve for support. The new diaphragm (lower view) is part #302563.

Figure 08-09
A look at the innards of a couple of early variations of the pressure tank.

EVINRUDE
SERVICE BULLETIN

Service Department
EVINRUDE MOTORS
Milwaukee 16, Wisconsin

NUMBER 199
April 21, 1952

LOW TYPE CRUIS-A-DAY TANK

We have received a few reports that the primer pump on the latest type squat or low type Cruis-a-Day tank does not deliver gas to the carburetor float bowl.

This trouble can nearly always be traced to a stuck check valve disc in the fuel tank foot valve #375846. This disc or check valve will sometimes stick due to a gum residue from the fuel.

Remove the foot valve assembly #375846 and soak the lower end in lacquer thinner until the disc loosens. When loose the disc will rattle when the foot valve is shaken.

Present day gasolines and oils have a certain amount of gum which may be precipitated out of the fuel mixture and may cause this condition.

EVINRUDE MOTORS

Bammann

Service Manager

Figure 08-10

A stuck check valve at the bottom of the fuel pick-up tube in a pressure tank is usually caused by old fuel which has been left in a tank for a long time, often years.

Evinrude
Service Bulletin

Service Department
EVINRUDE MOTORS
Milwaukee 16, Wisconsin

MISCELLANEOUS
NUMBER M-193
December 13, 1956

FUEL CONNECTOR REPAIR TOOLS
CRUIS-A-DAY FUEL SYSTEMS

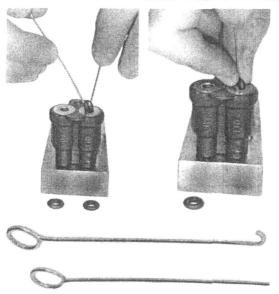

Here is a "do it yourself" tool project to save time in replacing fuel connector "O" rings. It does a good job whether used in the shop or field and the connector does not have to be disconnected from the fuel and air lines. The two wire tools and a few "O" rings fit a small envelope and make a neat repair kit. To make up your tools, cut two pieces of stiff wire (music or control cable wire) of #18 ga. (.0475 W & M) or #17 ga. (.054 W & M) diameter and 4" to 5" long. Round off and smooth the ends on both pieces. This will prevent damage to connector parts which will be explained later on. Next, bend a loop 3/8" to 1/2" diameter on one end of each wire for handles as shown above. This completes one tool.

On the remaining wire, form a hook with about 1/16" inside radius. Some may prefer a little larger or smaller hook, this one worked well.

To remove "O" rings:
Depress the valve plunger down into the connector body with the straight tool. Insert the hooked tool "flat" under the "O" ring, twist it "up" to catch the "O" ring and quickly pull it from its seat as shown above.

To replace "O" rings:
Put a drop or two of oil on the "O" ring and place on the connector face. Depress the valve plunger with the straight tool by passing it through the "O" ring as shown. Pinch the "O" ring together with your fingers and gently stuff it into position in its seat. Use the straight tool to position the "O" ring positively by pressing against the inside diameter of the "O" ring and moving the tool in a circular motion around the connector opening.

Be sure to check both valves for leaks before returning the fuel tanks to use.

EVINRUDE MOTORS
R. E. Burr
Service Promotion

Figure 08-11
Changing the O-rings is a tedious job requiring steady hand, a good eye, proper lighting, and a lot of patience. The only tools required are a couple of stiff paper clips (or similar wire) bent into the shapes shown.

FUEL TANK DRAIN PLUGS

To simplify total drainage of all Evinrude fuel tanks provision has been made by the utilization of the support plate to housing screws for this purpose.

The drain plugs on all 4 and 6 gallon Cruis-A-Day fuel tanks are the 2 screws immediately adjacent to and on the filler cap side of the hose connection. (see illustration #1)

The drain plug on the Cruis-A-Day Hi-Lift tank is the screw marked "drain". (see illustration #2)

Fuel should not be carried over from season to season and complete tank draining may be easily accomplished by removing the above mentioned screws and tipping the tank upside down.

Figure 08-12
Frequent draining of remote tanks helps eliminate accumulated water and other crud.

supplier Sierra. Remember that the tank must hold pressure to work. A pressure tank can also leak at the large rectangular cork gasket that the tank-top rests on, or around the tank-top mounting screws. There are little washer-like seals under these screw heads, which are easy to lose and difficult to find if you have lost yours. The tank can also leak through the cap. Check that the cap gasket is sealing.

Another item to check: note that the hose barbs on the tank are marked AIR and FUEL; Now note that the hose barbs on the quick-connect fitting are also marked AIR and FUEL. Are the connections reversed? If so, the engine is never going to run. When installing a new twin hose, fasten the hose to the tank but do not install the quick connector on the hose; depress the primer button several times (assuming there is some fuel in the tank) and

note which passage of the hose the fuel shoots out of; install the quick connect fitting on the hose with the hose barb marked FUEL connecting to the passage that the fuel shot from. Collect the spilled fuel in some sort of container for proper disposal.

Chances are the fuel tank you receive with an old engine will have old gasoline in it which would be best discarded. OMC remote fuel tanks, both the pressure tanks and the fuel pump tanks, had provisions made for draining (Figure 08-12). Unless you are SURE that the gasoline left in a tank is fresh and has the proper mix of oil in it, I would highly recommend that you dispose of the old fuel in an appropriate manner.

As to parts availability, a few parts for these tanks are available from Sierra, the after-market parts supplier. For example, the O-ring seals for the quick connector, OMC part #301824, are available as Sierra part #18-7111; the cork gasket which goes under the tank-top, OMC part #302557, is available as Sierra part #18-2887. The twin-passage hose is also available from Sierra, part #18-8051, but you have to buy it in a fifty-foot roll. A bit of calling around might find you a dealer selling it by the foot. The OMC part number for the earlier style diaphragm used in the remote tanks with a primer button consisting of aluminum button pinned to a small shaft is 302563: the part number for the diaphragm for the primer pump with a small black button is 376987.

As always, the internet can be a wonderful resource for locating parts for these engines.

9

Propellers

The propeller is what "connects" your outboard motor to the water. The proper propeller in good condition will give you the best performance out of your outboard. A damaged propeller, or one of incorrect size, can not only hurt performance, but can also damage the outboard (Figure 09-01).

Propeller size is expressed by two dimensions; diameter and pitch (Figure 09-02). The diameter of a two-blade propeller is the measurement, in inches, from the outer tip of one blade to the outer tip of the other. On a propeller with three or more blades, the diameter of the prop is the diameter of a circle that touches the outer tips of all of the blades. The pitch is the "angle" of the blades. The pitch is the measurement in inches of how far forward the prop would screw itself if it was rotated one full turn through a solid material.

Although there is usually little choice when it comes to the diameter of a proper for a particular outboard motor, often there is a much wider variety of pitches available. The pitch of a prop can be compared to the gearshift of an auto with a manual transmission. A low pitch or flat-pitch prop is comparable to low gear in the car; good for hauling heavy loads at low speed. A high pitch prop is the equivalent of

high gear in the car; it allows the auto to travel quickly without over speeding the engine. Just as you would not want to drive 70 mph on the highway in first gear and risk overspeeding the engine, you do not want to run a low pitch prop on a light boat with plenty of horsepower. Conversely, running a high pitch prop on a heavy boat with a relatively small outboard can lug the engine just as trying to drive the auto at low speeds in high gear will do. Lugging an engine can cause excessive wear and overheating.

People who deal with modern outboards, especially the larger engines, will discuss such things as blade area, blade rake, and other qualities of modern propellers, but we need not concern ourselves with such discussions when it comes to the older and smaller outboards.

New propellers are available from Johnson and Evinrude dealers and also from Michigan Wheel Corp. for just about all of the OMC-built outboards which are the subjects of this book. The choices of new propellers may be limited to only one or two for the smaller engines, but there is a wide selection of propellers available for the larger engines, say over about 10 HP.

A special note concerning the 10 HP outboards: the propellers used on 1957 and earlier models will not fit 1958 or later 10s due to a lower unit change. Conversely, the style of prop that will only fit 10s made earlier than 1958 will fit all OMC 12s, 15s, 18s & 20s from about 1953 until about 1970, and will also fit late-1960s 25s due to the similarities of the lower units on all of these models.

SERVICE PROMOTION

Johnson MOTORS

	✓
DEALER	
SERVICE MGR.	
SALES MGR.	
PARTS MGR.	
SERVICE MGR.	

April 11, 1962

SERVICE PROMOTION BULLETIN #312

SUBJECT: THE TRIED AND CONVICTED PROPELLER

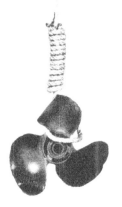

THE PROPELLER HERE

WAS TRIED AND CONVICTED AS A-
1. GAS ROBBER
2. PROMOTER OF ENGINE VIBRATION
3. SPARK PLUG USER
4. SPEED ROBBER
5. NERVE "WINDERUPPER"

JUST PLAIN LOUSY - AIN'T IT—
HOW'S YOUR PROPELLER DOIN'

To Ken Hauk, Service Manager, Sea-Horse, Inc., Punta Gorda, Florida goes credit for suggesting the proper handling of a faulty propeller – still in use, unbeknown perhaps to many boaters but still creating havoc until apprehended and appropriately sentenced.

If conditions are such that corrective measures and rehabilitation prove of no avail, it ought to be dealt with accordingly – just put away for keeps as Ken advises his owners by means of the poster.

It's a thought for your bulletin board customers' display too. Sometimes it takes the "out of ordinary" to drive a point home. The propeller here shown was justly convicted.

Sincerely

JOHNSON MOTORS

Jack Penland

Jack Penland
Service Promotion Manager

Figure 09-01
What this old Johnson Service Promotion Bulletin lacks in political correctness it makes up in effectiveness: a damaged propeller or a propeller of improper size can cause excessive fuel consumption and even damage the motor.

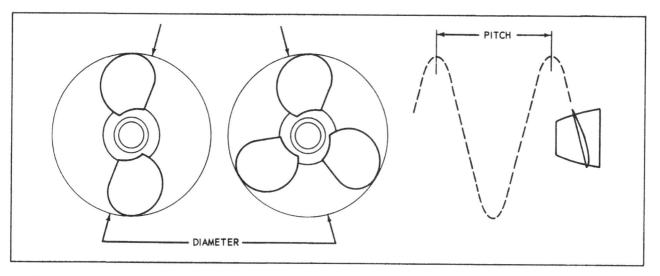

Figure 09-02
You will find little choice in the diameter of propellers for your outboard, but there may be a fairly wide selection of pitch available.

Used props are a common swap meet item but identifying exactly which props will fit your particular outboard can be problematic, as will be determining the diameter and pitch of a particular prop. Unlike props for inboard boats, which are usually stamped with the diameter and pitch, most outboard props are marked only with a part number. Used props may also have damage that is difficult to detect, such as an out-of-pitch blade or a "slipping" cushion hub. Another concern is that in 1956 the propellers and lower unit housings for almost all OMC models where modified to incorporate a fish line cutter to protect the propeller shaft seal from being damaged by fishing line wrapped around it (Figure 09-03). Although in most cases propellers for particular models can be swapped across this production change (i.e., a "line cutter" propeller can be used on a "non-line cutter" outboard, and also vice-versa), this is not always the case, and in any event the fish line cutter system will not work unless both the lower unit and the propeller have the cutter features.

New props for these older OMC outboards will always be made of aluminum, as will most used props you will run across. Occasionally you will run across bronze (not brass) props. These was a debate in the old days about whether running a bronze prop was harmful to the engine. The thought was that the weight and inertia of the heavier bronze propellers would damage the dog clutch in the lower unit. My opinion is that most dog clutch damage is caused by improper shifting technique—the engine should be "snapped" into gear, but not forced. Easing the engine into gear is what leads to excessive wear on the clutch dog and gear engagement faces, although the increased inertia of the heavier bronze prop probably does not help the situation.

OMC used several different methods of attaching the prop to the propeller shaft (Figure 09-04). The little 3 HP models had a threaded prop nut covered with a "snap-on" rubber nose cone, although often the nose

Evinrude
Service Bulletin

Service Department
EVINRUDE MOTORS
Milwaukee 16, Wisconsin

MISCELLANEOUS
NUMBER M-191
December 10, 1956

WEED AND LINE CUTTER
ALL MODELS

About midway through the 1956 production year, a weed and line cutter was added on all Evinrude motor models to prevent damage to gear case and propeller by weed and line winding around them.

Notches were added to the leading edge of the propeller hub and a notched ring was added to the gear case as shown.

The propeller notches pick up the weeds or line and sheer them against the notched ring on the gear case.

SAFTI-GRIP CLUTCH PROPELLER
MODEL: Sportwin, Fastwin, Big Twin & Lark

At the same time, the weed and line cutter was added to all models, a new propeller and drive pin was introduced on the above mentioned models only, to eliminate shearing of pins and reduce propeller damage.

The new propeller and steel drive pin react to shock the same as before, but when excessive shock is encountered, the steel drive pin holds permitting the new propeller hub to absorb the shock to safe limits. When the maximum shock load point is reached, the new hub permits the propeller to slip momentarily on its shaft before damage or breakage can occur.

Refer to following Service Bulletins for individual model propeller installations.

EVINRUDE MOTORS

R. E. Burr

Service Promotion

Figure 09-03   The fish line cutter was intended to protect the propeller shaft seal which is easily damaged by fish line wrapped around the propeller shaft. The cushioned propeller hub was intended to protect the propeller and drive train from the shock of an impact without temporarily disabling the engine as a broken shear pin would. Outboards using the cushioned hub propellers used a much stronger "drive pin" rather than a shear pin.

Service Department
EVINRUDE MOTORS
Milwaukee 16, Wisconsin

MISCELLANEOUS
Number M-222
November 5, 1957

PROPELLER NUTS

ALL MODELS

There are four (4) types of propeller nuts in use on 1958 Evinrudes:

1. Big Twins, Lark, Four-Fifty and Starflite use a molded nylon <u>Push-on</u> type of propeller nut and cotter pin. <u>DO NOT USE A WRENCH ON THESE NUTS.</u>

2. Sportwins and Fastwins use a molded nylon threaded nut and cotter pin.

3. Fisherman and Fleetwin use a cotter pin to retain the propeller and a rubber spinner cap to retain the drive pin.

4. Lightwin uses a brass nut, cotter pin and rubber cap.

<u>DO NOT</u> draw propeller nuts tight against the inner hub on Models having threaded type nuts. "Back off" rather than "pull up" on the nut to align cotter pin holes. Too tight a propeller nut prevents normal operation of the drive pin.

Refer to Bulletin No. M-189 before installing any propeller.

EVINRUDE MOTORS

Service Promotion

R. E. Burr
mi

Figure 09-04
For whatever reason, the method of mounting the propeller varied from model to model.

cone is missing. The 5½s and 7½s had the snap-on rubber nose cone but no threaded prop nut; the prop was held on by the shear pin while the nose cone kept the shear pin in place. The 10s through 20s had threaded nose cones secured with a cotter pin, as did the 25s and 30s from the early and mid 1950s. The 35 HP model introduced in 1957 featured a plastic "slip-on" nose cone secured with a cotter pin. Many of these plastic nose cones have been broken by people who put a wrench on them thinking that they were threaded.

The shear pin is located at the aft (prop nut) end of the propeller on some motors and at the forward (lower unit) end of other models. So just what is a shear pin? It is a metal pin that locks the prop to the spinning propeller shaft and which is intended to "shear" or break should the prop come into contact with a hard object such as a log or rock. This allows the propeller to spin free on the shaft, hopefully sparing the prop or other engine components from damage. The shear pin is intended to be a sacrificial weak link.

In the mid 1950s, however, "cushioned hub" propellers were introduced (Figure 09-03). These props had a rubber-mounted hub which was intended to absorb the impact of a hit. The props continued to be locked to the prop shaft with a pin, but now it was a much stronger pin and the factory referred to it as a "drive pin" and not a "shear pin."

Although with some searching a genuine shear pin or drive pin for a particular model can be found, few people go to the trouble. Often pieces of nails or other material will be found in place of the proper pin. My own method is to purchase brass rod of the proper diameter at a hardware store or hobby shop and to use a hacksaw to cut pins of the correct length. The brass is somewhat more prone to breakage than a proper shear pin, and is definitely weaker than a steel drive pin. I just consider this extra protection for the prop and engine.

Keep in mind, however, that a broken shear pin in the wrong situation could put your boat and its passengers in danger, so the weakness of a substitute brass pin could be a safety issue. I always make it a point to carry spare pins and I usually carry a spare prop as well. I have had the rubber hub of a cushioned hub propeller fail, allowing the body of the prop to slide on the hub and reducing the top speed of the boat to about one mile per hour. It would have been a long six-mile trip back to the launch ramp if I had not had a spare prop in the boat. If you are going to carry a spare consider having one of a different size than your regular propeller. That way you can have a "speed" prop for light loads and a "power" prop for heavy loads.

Improper tightening of the threaded propeller nuts can lead to shear pin breakage, and can also cause damage to the propeller or even the shaft. Models that use the threaded propeller nuts have a slot machined into the forward face of the propeller hub that the shear pin/ drive pin engages. If the propeller nut is too lose, there will be excessive slack between the pin and the slot which will cause the slot to wear and enlarge, permanently damaging the hub of the propeller Figure 09-05). Improper tightening of a threaded propeller nut can also cause damage to the rubber cushioned hub itself (Figure 09-06). When installing a pro-

Johnson MOTORS Service Bulletin

DEALER
SERVICE MGR.
SALES MGR.
PARTS MGR.
SERVICE MGR.

June 8, 1959

SERVICE BULLETIN NO. SB–718

SUBJECT: SECURING THE 10 and 18 H.P. PROPELLER NUT.

The stainless steel drive pin used in the 10 and 18 H.P. propeller will wear the inner hub of the propeller, as shown, to the point of complete failure if the propeller nut is not tightened properly.

This type of wear, resulting in propeller failure, can be overcome by securely tightening the propeller nut. Secure the propeller nut in the following manner.

Insert the drive pin in the propeller shaft, and place the propeller in position. Install the propeller nut, and secure as tightly as possible by hand. With a wrench, advance the nut until the cotter pin hole is in alignment. (DO NOT BACK THE NUT OFF TO ALIGN THE COTTER PIN HOLE).

The propeller secured in this manner, will not allow the drive pin to float causing hub damage.

JOHNSON MOTORS

Jack Penland
Service Department

Figure 09-05
Improperly tightening the threaded propeller nuts some models used can lead to damage to the propeller hub. Be sure to check the hubs of used propellers for enlarged and worn drive pin slots. Also, note that the factory changed their recommended procedure for tightening prop nuts from what it was in Figure 09-04.

EVINRUDE
SERVICE BULLETIN

Service Department
EVINRUDE MOTORS
Milwaukee 16, Wisconsin

LIGHTWIN
NUMBER 3.-3
MAY 10, 1954

TIGHTENING PROPELLER NUT 43A71 ON THE LIGHTWIN

Tightening the propeller nut 43A71 on the Lightwin is of considerable importance. The nut should be screwed on as tightly as possible, using the fingers. Then continue with a wrench to the next alignment of the cotter pin hole. Insert the cotter pin, and the nut is then properly adjusted.

If less tension is placed on this propeller nut, there is a tendency of the propeller itself to wobble in its rubber mountings. It is also probable that the slip clutch will not function properly.

Tightening the propeller nut as specified above will assure you of proper propeller and clutch action.

EVINRUDE MOTORS

Herb Dickerson

H. Dickerson   Service Promotion Manager

Figure 09-06
The function of the rubber shock-absorbing hub on some models can be affected by how tightly the propeller nut is tightened.

peller on an outboard, it is usually a good idea to grease the shaft to guard against corrosion and wear (Figure 09-07).

Occasionally someone will bring up the subject of "test wheels." These are special propellers used by mechanics to run outboards in test tanks (Figure 09-08). Since the typical test tank provides very poor flow of water to the propeller, an engine run at high rpms in a test tank will often surge faster and slower as the propeller alternately "bites" the water and then loses its bite. This surging can make testing and adjusting an outboard difficult. Test wheels are designed to properly load the engine in test tank conditions but to produce no forward thrust, eliminating the surging. A

Evinrude
Service Bulletin

Service Department
EVINRUDE MOTORS
Milwaukee 16, Wisconsin

MISCELLANEOUS
NUMBER M-155
January 11, 1956

SHOP INSTALLATION OF PROPELLERS

To reduce the possibility of excessive wear in the propeller hub and on the propeller shaft, it is important that both the hub, propeller shaft and threaded end be coated liberally with Lubriplate #930 AA grease, Perfect Seal #4, or other non-drying cement of similar characteristics.

Silt and sand particles find their way into the area between the propeller hub and shaft to cause premature wear.

Refer to Service Bulletin M-48 to check where to purchase Lubriplate #930 AA, also Bulletin M-73 where to purchase Perfect Seal #4.

EVINRUDE MOTORS

Service Manager

F. J. Bammann
bcm

Figure 09-07   Greasing the propeller shaft before installing the propeller is always a good idea on these old outboards, especially if you intend to run in salt water.

test wheel can not be used to propel a boat, and is an object that you will probably never run across. You should be aware, however, that running your outboard in gear with its standard propeller in a 55 gal drum of water, for example, will cause this same surging and it is not necessarily indicative of a problem with the engine. Also remember that an outboard that is run for long periods of time in a test tank can easily overheat.

Johnson MOTORS

SERVICE PROMOTION

January 26, 1961

SERVICE PROMOTION BULLETIN #273

SUBJECT: WHY A TEST WHEEL FOR TANK TESTING

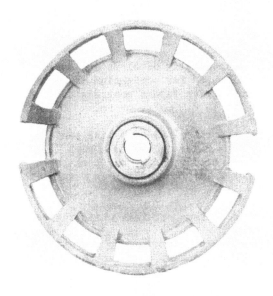

The function of final testing and tuning of any Outboard Motor is best performed under actual contions – on a boat in open water where all conditions of normal operation may be observed. But, it's not always possible or convenient to do so because of the time consumed and more often, inaccessability to waters edge – thus, the propeller test wheel for tank use.

It is a known fact that propeller thrust, the force required to drive the boat, is greatest at full throttle between the time the boat starts to move and the instant at which it breaks over to assume planing position – point of greatest thrust. On having reached the planing position, propeller thrust for a moment falls off abruptly but commences to gradually build up again as boat speed accelerates and engine R.P.M. approaches the range established for best performance – normal operation for the particular unit.

With this in mind, each of the available Johnson propeller test wheels, have been designed, constructed and calibrated for each specific model horse power range to simulate in the test tank, as nearly as possible, thrust and load condition approximating those encountered during normal over-all performance of the motor and at which time all final adjustments and tuning should be accomplished for maximum results.

Any attempt to check out or tune a motor laboring at low RPM in the shop test tank because of the "regular" propeller installation is futile and wasted effort which serves no purpose. R.P.M. must be "up" to correctly perform required adjustments – particularly so, the slow and high speed carburetor needle settings.

In view of the high speed needles having been removed from the 1961 RD and V4 series carburetors and replaced with fixed jets, test tank running within the desired R.P.M. range becomes significantly important since the jets are calibrated accordingly for best performance.

See test wheel performance chart enclosed and the list of propeller test wheels below.

Minimum desired R.P.M. shown for each model is average minimum for test running with the properly designated test wheel installed at 600 feet above sea level (Waukegan, Illinois) in a tank 60" x 60" x 40" filled to approximately 565 gallons water capacity.

Figure 09-08
Test wheels are something you are not likely to run across, and are really something you can live without, but this is their function.

10

Lower Units

~

If you are a perfectionist, you are not going to like what I am about to say. I suggest that living with imperfection will simplify your life. I am talking about tolerating a lower unit that allows a little water to leak in. I suggest that a willingness to frequently change the lower unit lubricant (say, after every three or four outings) might be less of a hassle than trying to re-seal an old lower unit.

Seal kits are available from Sierra for these old OMC outboards, but consider this: some of these outboards require special tools (or "jury-rigged" tools) to change some of the seals involved. A damaged propellor shaft, scored by having fishing line wrapped around it, will probably damage a new prop shaft seal and cause it to leak. Worn bearings on the propeller shaft or vertical drive shaft may not be bad enough to disable the engine but may allow the shaft to "wobble" so much that it tears up the new seal. Stocking up on cheap lower unit oil from a discount store and frequently checking the lubricant for water and changing it when it becomes contaminated might be a viable option for a lower unit that does not leak too badly. If it leaks like a sieve, however, then an attempt at resealing is probably warranted, but don't be surprised if it still leaks a bit afterwards.

Starting with the basics, changing the lower unit lubricant is a simple, albeit messy job that *anyone* can do. Little in the way of tools is required (Figure 10-01). The oil is drained by removing two plugs from the lower unit (Figure10-02).

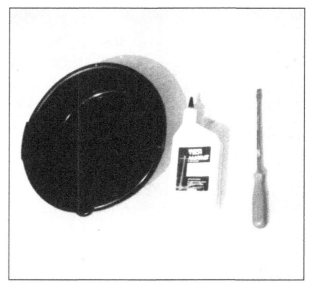

Figure 10-01   The only items needed to change the lower unit lubricant are fresh lubricant, a drain pan of some sort, and a large flat-head screwdriver. Also several rags or paper towels to clean up the inevitable mess.

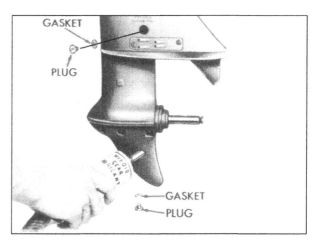

Figure 10-02
After draining the old lubricant, fresh lube is injected into the drain (bottom) hole until it flows out of the vent (upper) hole. Note the little gaskets on the drain plugs.

NOTE; there is a screw, much smaller than the drain plugs, located near the very bottom of the lower unit that is actually a pivot pin for part of the shift linkage (Figure 10-12). This pivot pin screw usually has a Phillips-head, while the drain and vent plugs always use a large slotted-head screwdriver. *Do not confuse this pivot pin screw with the drain plugs.* If you should manage to accidentally remove the pivot pin screw, immediately try to reinstall it and DON'T TOUCH THE SHIFT LEVER UNTIL THE PIN IS BACK IN. If you are lucky, the bell crank that rides on the pivot pin will not have slipped out of position and the pin will go back in without trouble. With the pin back in, try shifting the engine, keeping in mind that you must slowly turn the propeller or the flywheel to allow the engine to engage the gears; do not force the lever. If the gears do not engage, then the bell crank slipped out of position and you will have to remove the pivot pin screw and, using a good light and an awl (or long nail or something similar), try to pry the bell crank back into position. Its hole must be aligned with the hole in the housing so that the pivot pin can be reinserted.

With both the drain and vent plugs removed, allow the oil to fully drain. Catch the oil in some type of container and inspect it for the presence of water (Figure 10-03). Compare the oil that drains out to the new oil; lower unit oil that resembles a vanilla milkshake is contaminated with water. Sometimes, clear water will drain out. While the lower unit is draining, check to see that both the drain plug and the vent plug have little washer-like gaskets on them. Missing or damaged plug gaskets may

Figure 10-03
Inspect the drained lubricant for the presence of water, which will either flow out of the lubricant separately or combine with the lube to form a "milkshake."

be the cause of your leaking lower unit. New gaskets (Sierra part #18-2945) are under a buck apiece as of this writing. That pivot pin screw should also have a gasket under its head. Partially loosening it without fully removing it should allow you to check to see if its gasket is in place. This seal is only available from a dealer, but is less likely to be bad or missing.

To refill the lower unit with oil, insert the nozzle of the lower unit lubricant tube or quart bottle into the bottom hole and squeeze oil in until it runs out the upper hole. While holding the bottle or tube in place in the lower hole,

EVINRUDE
Service Bulletin

Service Department
EVINRUDE MOTORS
Milwaukee 16, Wisconsin

LUBRICATION
BULLETIN NO. 379
JULY 1, 1960

GEAR CASE CAPACITIES

Occasionally we receive requests for the gear case capacities of late model engines. The following list shows the amount of oil and the approximate number of tubes required to fill each of them.

OMC Type "B" is recommended for all models.

H.P.	MODEL	YEAR OF MFG.	CAPACITY (oz.)	APPROX. NO. OF TUBES TO FILL
3	Lightwin	1952-1960	2.9	1/3
5½	Fisherman	1954-1960	8.2	1 plus
7½	Fleetwin	1954-1958	8.6	1 plus
10	Sportwin	1958-1960	8.6	1 plus
18	Fastwin	1957-1960	8.1	1 plus
35-40	Big Twin & Lark	1957-1960	13.7	1 3/4 plus
50	Starflite & Four-Fifty	1958-1959	34.8	4 1/3 plus
75	Starflite II	1960	21.5	2 1/2 plus

OMC Type "B" is available from your parts distributor packaged as follows:

#378111 - 1 gallon can (Packed 6 to a carton) - - - - $ 5.00 per gallon
#378112 - 8 oz. tubes (Packed 12 to a carton)- - - - 12.00 per carton

EVINRUDE MOTORS

Richard Bayley

Richard Bayley
Service Promotion
Manager

Figure 10-04
The lower unit lubricant capacities of older OMC outboard motors.

install the upper plug. Then quickly remove the tube or bottle from the lower hole and install the lower plug. Yes, this is a messy job, and no, you cannot refill from the upper hole as you may not get the lower unit completely full (Figure 10-04).

I always purchase lower unit oil at a discount store. Since most of my lower units leak a bit of water and require that the oil be frequently changed, I try to buy the cheapest oil available. About any lower unit oil on the shelf at a discount store will work just fine in older OMC outboards. I don't even bother to check what "type" of lower unit oil it is. The exception would be for an electric shift lower unit, which requires a special lower unit oil. But I have already advised against buying an outboard with electric shift.

One other comment—there is a white grease (not oil; grease is thicker than oil) sold as a lower unit lubricant for outboard motors without a full gearshift lower unit, such as the little Johnson and Evinrude 3 HP models and the 5 HP models sold for just a few years in the 1960s. This grease is called Lubriplate #105 grease and while it is normally only recommended for the non-shift engines, it has been used in full gearshift engines with very leaky lower units. The heavy grease is much less likely to wash out than oil, although water can still leak in. After use, the drain plugs can be removed, the water allowed to drain out for several hours, and then the grease can be topped-off rather than totally replaced. With the Lubriplate #105 you do not have to be as concerned with having all of the lubricant leak out of the lower unit, leaving nothing but

water. But, using the grease in a shift lower unit is akin to using very heavy motor oil in a worn auto engine in an attempt to maintain oil pressure. It is generally considered poor practice. But whether we are talking about an old car or an old outboard, if you are not expecting too many more hours/miles of use, it will work. Lubriplate #105 is also used when assembling automotive engines after rebuilding and it can usually be found at a good auto parts store.

No matter what lubricant you use, be sure to drain and refill the lower unit before the onset of freezing weather to avoid the possibility of water in the lower unit freezing and breaking the aluminum housing. If you are using Lubriplate #105, the grease will not drain; leave the plugs out for a few hours to be sure that the water has drained, and top-off with more grease. Leaving a lower unit sit all winter with no lubricant in it risks corrosion of the shafts and gears, and also of the roller or ball bearings in engines that have them.

The "transmission" that gives you forward, neutral, and reverse is located in the lower unit (Figure10-05). Outboards use a dog clutch which works as follows: there is a small pinion gear mounted on the bottom of the vertical drive shaft, and which is always in engagement with the forward and reverse gears, which ride on the horizontal propellor shaft but which are free to rotate independently of the prop shaft. Also on the prop shaft, between the forward and reverse gears, is the dog clutch, which is splined (locked) to the prop shaft. The shift linkage moves this dog clutch forward in order

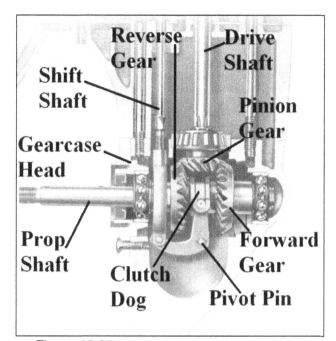

Figure 10-05
The general arrangement of parts in a gear shift lower unit.

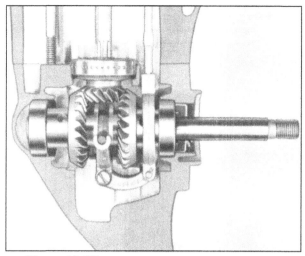

Figure10-07
Neutral position.

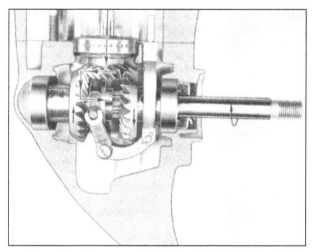

Figure 10-06
Forward gear engaged.

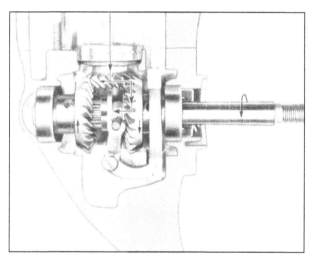

Figure 10-08
Reverse engaged. Note that the all gears are always engaged; the shift is effected by locking free-wheeling gears to the prop shaft.

to engage forward gear (Figure10-06), to the center position to provide neutral (Figure 10-07), and rearward to engage reverse (Figure 10-08). All gears are always engaged with each other; the shift is made by the dog clutch locking one gear or the other to the prop shaft instead of allowing the gear to rotate freely on the prop shaft.

A gear shift lower unit that jumps out of gear has a problem that must be addressed immediately or severe damage could occur, if it has not already. Often, the reason for an engine jumping or slipping out of gear is a worn or incorrectly adjusted shift linkage. The linkage adjustment is made at a bolt on the shift lever on the side of the engine (Figure 10-09). Be sure not to

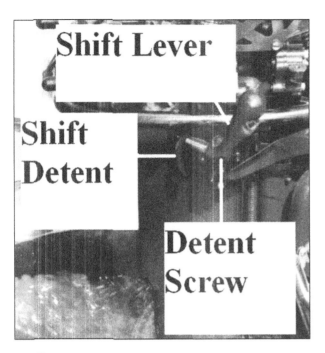

Figure 10-09
Shift lever adjustment point.

force a non-running outboard motor into gear (Figure 10-10) as the engagement lugs on the clutch dog and gears may not be in alignment. It might be necessary to slowly turn the flywheel or the propeller a bit in order to allow the gears to engage. If you try to force them, you will damage the linkage. Remember to rotate the flywheel clockwise only.

Most of these outboards (the 5½ being an exception) have a spring-loaded detent which acts upon the shift lever to hold the engine in gear. When I adjust the linkage on these engines, I like to set them up so that the strength of the detent spring is forcing the shift lever to the "forward gear" position. In other words, I want the shift linkage to bottom-out in the forward gear position before the detent bottoms out in the forward position. This is done by shifting the engine into forward gear (with the engine not running, of course; disconnect the spark plug wires as a safety precaution), then

loosen the adjusting bolt and move the gearshift lever just *slightly* towards the neutral position while not allowing the rest of linkage to move, then tightening up the adjustment bolt. Adjusting the linkage in this manner means that the linkage is in full forward gear but that the spring-loaded detent is still trying to force the gearshift further forward. If the linkage is a little worn, adjusting it in this manner will help to hold the engine in forward gear, possibly at the expense of reverse. While an engine that jumps or slips out of forward gear should not be run, jumping out of reverse is not as big of a concern as reverse gear is used much less often than forward, and at much slower speeds. The ideal situation of course is an engine that stays in both forward and reverse gear with no jumping.

If the engine is jumping out of gear and the linkage is adjusted correctly and is not overly worn or loose, then the problem is most likely in the lower unit and it will have to be disassembled. Odds are the clutch dog has worn or chipped teeth (Figure 10-11), and/or the forward and reverse gears have worn/chipped engagement lugs for the clutch dog. Start by draining the oil out of the lower unit. Although the lower unit can be disassembled without removing it from the rest of the engine, I prefer to remove the lower unit and clamp it upside down in a vise (padded well) or by clamping the anti-cavitation plate to the edge of the work bench. Either way, shift the engine into reverse before beginning the tear-down.

Remove the propellor and the pivot pin screw that I mentioned earlier. Next, remove the six or eight screws which hold the bottom

EVINRUDE
SERVICE BULLETIN

Service Department
EVINRUDE MOTORS
Milwaukee 16, Wisconsin

MISCELLANEOUS
NUMBER M-22
May 4, 1953

SHIFTING GEARS

Unless the operator is sure the gears are in proper position, the gears on an Evinrude motor, with gear shift control, should not be shifted when motor is not running.

If, when shifting, the clutch dog bosses do not engage the indentations in the gear hub; there is a possibility of bending the shift rod or other parts, and throwing the shift mechanism out of adjustment.

Should you try to shift gears in an idle motor and the shifter mechanism not engage readily, rotate the propeller wheel until the clutch dog engages the notches in the gear hub.

Do not try to force the shifter mechanism. The gears must engage readily.

It will be a help to your owners if you will instruct them accordingly.

EVINRUDE MOTORS

F.J. Bammann

Service Manager

Figure 10-10
Care must be taken when attempting to shift a non-running engine into gear.

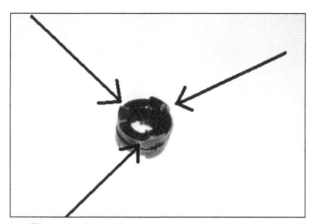

Figure 10-11
Dog clutch showing chipped and worn engagement lugs. The engine this dog clutch was removed from was jumping out of gear. Damage was most likely caused by improper linkage adjustment or improper shifting by the operator.

(top, with the lower unit upside down) of the lower unit on; the half with the skeg (fin) on it. Slowly and carefully lift bottom of the lower unit up off the other half of the housing. You should now be looking at all of the gears and shafts and other innards of the lower unit (Figure 10-12). This would be a very good time to start taking photos and making written notes of exactly how everything goes back together (Figure 10-13).

The larger big twin engines will have replaceable roller and/or ball bearings on the prop shaft while smaller engines have their prop shafts running in bronze bushings that

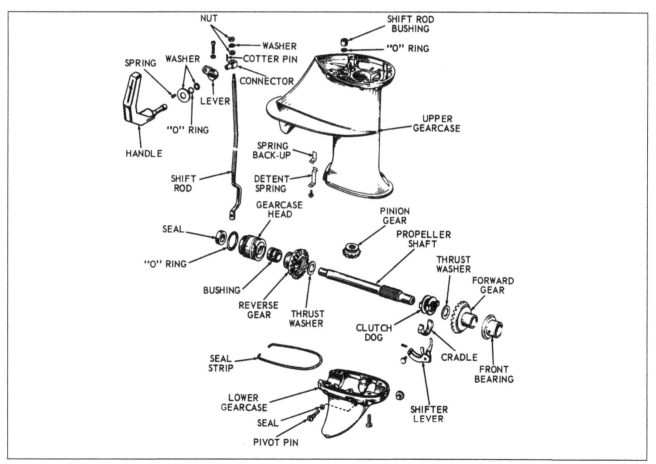

Figure 10-12   Diagram of lower unit "transmission" and shift linkage for a smaller OMC outboard; larger outboards are similar with the exceptions that they have roller and ball bearings instead of bushings, and that there is a disconnect in the vertical shift shaft for removing the lower unit.

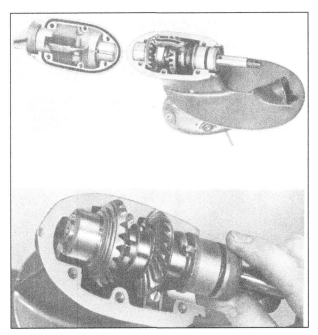

Figure 10-13
Lower unit of a smaller outboard upside-down and opened up.

are often cast into the housings and that are not replaceable. Other than that, all of these lower units look pretty much alike. Note the forward and reverse gears on the prop shaft and the dog clutch on the prop shaft between the two gears. You can lift the whole shaft up out of the housing but be alert that parts do not fall off of it. Check the engagement lugs on the dog clutch and also the corresponding lugs on the faces of the gears. Rounded or chipped edges on these lugs are a problem. Damage to these lugs is almost always caused by either improper adjustment of the shift linkage or by improper shifting technique by the motor's operator (Figure 10-14 & 10-15). Outboard motors should be shifted crisply, and not "eased" into gear. Do not ever force an outboard into gear, however. An outboard motor being shifted too slowly will usually emit a rattling noise which is caused by the engagement lugs bouncing off each other

before fully engaging. This bouncing of the lugs is what causes the damage.

If excess wear is limited to the forward lugs on the clutch dog, often the dog can be removed from the shaft and turned around so that forward gear is now being engaged with the former reverse lugs on the clutch dog. This will probably cause the engine to jump out of gear in reverse now, but reverse if used much less often than forward gear and at much lower speeds. The best solution would be a new clutch dog, but that might not be available or if available might cost more than the motor is worth. Another option is used parts but be sure to inspect used parts to be sure they are in better shape than what you removed.

If the engagement lugs on the gears are rounded and/or chipped, or if the gear teeth are damaged, you will need new gears, or maybe another lower unit. Or you may elect to set the engine aside for use as a parts engine and seek a better specimen of the same or a similar model. If the cast-in bronze bushings are worn, you will need to find another housing. It should be noted that a good machine shop could repair the chipped/worn clutch dog and gears, as well as the worn bushings in the housing, but if you have to pay retail price for the machine work you are going to end up with a very expensive engine.

If you have torn down the lower unit to correct leaks, there are several areas that could be responsible. The propeller shaft seal is the most obvious place. Fishing line wrapped around the propeller shaft is a common seal-killer. The prudent outboarder will frequently

EVINRUDE
Service Bulletin

Service Department
EVINRUDE MOTORS
Milwaukee 16, Wisconsin

TROUBLE SHOOTING
BULLETIN NO. 428
JANUARY 15, 1961

COMPLAINTS OF PREMATURE GEAR AND SHIFTER CLUTCH DOG WEAR

Wear of gear and clutch dog ears can be very much accelerated by operators who have the mistaken belief that gentle shifting (easing into gear) is the proper practice to safeguard the shifting mechanism and the engine in general. This idea is particularly prevalent in the minds of operators who are new and un-iniated to outboarding. Actually, the thought is completely wrong, because easing into gear causes the ears of gears and clutch dogs to rap and slide off their edges many times during one shift maneuver before the gears finally engage. This repeated rapping-and-sliding-off process is the direct and principle cause of accelerated gear wear, as well as the cause of their chipping.

Figure 1

Figure #1 illustrates a shifter clutch dog and gears which were claimed to be prematurely worn because of a slight rounding of the ears, indicated by the short slim highlight on the top edges (arrows). This slight amount of wear is normal, even though the operators shifting practice is ideal, that is, smartly snapped-shifted, instead of easing into gear, and does not indicate faulty material, parts, or workmanship.

Figure 2

Figure #2 illustrates a chipped ear on a clutch dog (arrow). Since this clutch dog was fully engaging the gears as intended, (note contact area indicated by highlight between arrows - upper right hand ear) shift linkage was correctly adjusted. The chipping in this case was caused by the rapping-and-sliding-off process previously mentioned and was due to faulty shifting practice by the operator. This clutch dog should not be reused, but should be replaced at customer expense, not under warranty, as there is no indication of faulty material or workmanship. Also, the stained appearance of this particular clutch dog, indicates its being used for a considerably longer time than is allowed by warranty.

- over -

Figures 10-14 & 10-15 Improper shifting technique by the outboard motor's operator can lead to major damage.

Correct shifting practices are a <u>must</u>, however, to be most effective gear shift linkage on the engine <u>should</u> <u>first</u> be checked as prescribed in the service manual, lower unit data Bulletin 5-27. If linkage is not in accordance with this bulletin, make the necessary adjustments.

After a linkage check and adjustment has been made on the engine, be certain to also check the nurled adjusting nut on the remote shift cable, if used, so the lock pin aligns with the hole in the shift lever when in neutral position. Double check this lock pin alignment in forward and reverse gears also, to be certain of full and complete gear engagement with remote operation.

The final step in reducing accelerated gear and clutch dog wear, is to advise your customers that the "Do-and-Don't" rules of shifting Evinrude engines are these:

1. DO shift only at recommended idle speeds (600 RPM plus or minus 100).

2. <u>DO</u> <u>smartly</u> <u>snap</u> <u>shift</u> (a quick snappy movement of the lever to its full limit of travel).

3. DON'T shift above recommended idle speeds.

4. <u>DON'T</u> <u>ease</u> into gear.

5. <u>DON'T</u> <u>slam</u> into gear.

EVINRUDE MOTORS

Richard Bayley

Service Promotion
Manager

check the lower unit for fishing line. The prop shaft seal can be removed from the gearcase head by driving it out. There may be two small holes in the gearcase head allowing the seal to be driven out with a punch and a hammer. Otherwise, some type of puller will be needed. Pay attention to which face of the old seal faces forward, and gently tap the new seal into place. If you bought a seal kit, you will have a new O-ring to put around the gear case head. So you might as well remove the old O-ring and clean its groove, taking care not to nick the surface. A light coating of gasket sealer on the groove would not hurt.

Another potential leak is the vertical drive shaft seal located under the water pump. To replace this seal, you will need to remove the water pump housing, impeller key and wear plate. At this point the drive shaft should lift right out of the lower unit unless you have one of the few models which have a snap ring holding the pinion gear onto the bottom of the shaft. In this case, you will need to remove the snap ring with a pair of snap ring pliers. Once the drive shaft is out, remove the seal from the housing with a puller of some sort or by carefully prying it out. Tap in the new seal and slide the drive shaft back in making sure it is fully seated in its pinion gear. Install the pump wear plate, impeller key, impeller, and pump housing.

Another source of leaks is the seal around the shift shaft. This is an O-ring which is held in the housing by a retainer that must be driven out with a round rod of the proper diameter. (Or the special tool which you don't have, of course.)

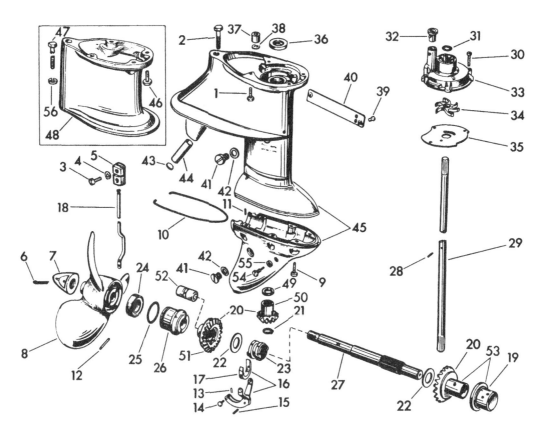

INDEX TO PARTS
(In order of disassembly)

1 Upper gear housing to exhaust housing screw
2 Exhaust housing to gear case screw, rear
3 Shift rod connector screw
4 Shift rod connector screw lockwasher
5 Upper and lower shift rod connector
6 Propeller nut cotter pin
7 Propeller nut
8 Propeller and bushing
9 Gear housing screw
10 Upper to lower gear case seal
11 Front and rear bearing dowel
12 Propeller drive pin
13 Yoke to pin cotter pin
14 Yoke to shift rod pin
15 Shifter lever pivot pin (where used)
16 Shifter lever and cradle assy.
17 Cradle
18 Shift rod, lower
19 Front bearing
20 Set of gears
21 Pinion retaining ring
22 Propeller shaft thrust washer
23 Clutch dog shifter assy.
24 Propeller shaft seal
25 Gear case head "O" ring
26 Gear housing head and seal assy.
27 Propeller shaft
28 Pump impeller pin
29 Drive shaft
*Used on 1960 Models & up.

30 Impeller housing to upper gear housing screw
31 Drive shaft to crankshaft "O" ring
32 Water tube grommet, lower
33 Impeller housing
34 Water pump impeller
35 Impeller housing plate
36 Drive shaft seal
37 Shift rod bushing, lower
38 Lower shift rod seal "O" ring
39 Water by-pass cover screw
40 Water by-pass cover
41 Oil plug
42 Oil plug washer
43 Water intake screen plug
44 Water intake screen
45 Gear case, upper and lower
46 Gear housing to gear case extension screw,
     5 inches longer
47 Exhaust housing to gear case extension screw,
     rear, 5 inches longer
48 Gear case extension, 5 inches longer
49 Pinion thrust washer
50 Drive shaft pinion
51 Rear reversing gear
52 Rear reversing gear bushing
53 Gear and bushing assembly, front
54 Shifter lever pivot pin
55 Shifter lever pivot pin washer
*56 Lockwasher

Figure 10-16   Parts diagram for the typical gear shift lower unit.

Johnson MOTORS

WAUKEGAN, ILLINOIS

Service Bulletin

	✓
DEALER	
SERVICE MGR.	
SALES MGR.	
PARTS MGR.	
SERVICE MGR.	

May 11, 1961

Bulletin No. SB-845
Gearcases

SUBJECT: Gearcase leakage prevention;
      5½ thru 50 h.p. engines (CD thru V-50 model series)
      <u>Additional references:</u>
      5½ thru 40 h.p. series - P. 192-27 of Gen. Service Manual.
      V-50 series - P. 110 of V-4 Service Manual.

For the purpose of discussing gearcase leakage problems, the 40 h.p. model RD-23 is used as an example. Except for specific part number references, the following assembly procedure is also applicable to the 5½, 7½, 10, 15, 18, 25, 30, 35 and 50 h.p. engines because these have similar gearcase designs and therefore require the same basic assembly procedure and precautions.

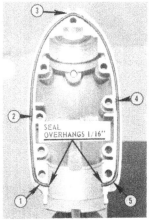

Illustrating overhang & cementing points with seal against outer edge of groove.

FIG. 1

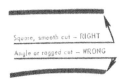

Illustrating proper cutting of seal's ends.

Gearcase leakage correction and prevention is first of all primarily a matter of carefully cutting seal #302604 to the proper length followed by careful installation in the skeg's groove with liberal application of Marprox Sealer 1000. The 'spaghetti' seal, as gearcase seal 302604 is sometimes called, must, without stretching, be placed against the outer edge of the groove and must also overhang the groove's ends about 1/16th inch (no more!) on both sides so the seal's ends will <u>squarely</u> butt against housing 303050 without causing the seal to buckle, figure 1. Be sure to cut the seal ends <u>square</u> - not at an angle! (figure 2). The square cut, and butt, is very important because the smallest space between housing 303050 and the ends of the seal will permit lubricant leakage. Neither must the seal be permitted to buckle because this is also apt to allow leakage.

With the seal properly cut to length with <u>square</u> ends, and correctly located at the outer edge of the skeg's groove,
1. Spot cement the seal at five (5) points to hold it in position, (numbered arrows, figure 1).
2. Apply a liberal amount of Marprox Sealer 1000 over the entire mounting surface <u>on the upper gearcase</u>, and another touch-up application at both ends of the spaghetti seal and around the bends at points 1 and 5 on the skeg, figure 1.
3. To minimize disturbance of the seal in positioning the skeg on the upper gearcase, insert a gearcase screw in each of the Skeg's three (3) screw-holes at points 1, 3 and 5, figure 1. These screws serve as guides and assist in more readily positioning the skeg.
4. Assemble the upper gearcase and skeg, but be sure not to displace the spaghetti seal. GIVE SPECIAL ATTENTION TO THE OVERHANGING SEAL ENDS TO BE CERTAIN THEY WILL SQUARELY BUTT AGAINST HOUSING 303050. DO NOT PERMIT THEM TO BECOME PINCHED, OR WEDGED, BETWEEN THE SKEG AND THIS HOUSING!!!

5. Screw in the three (3) guide screws just far enough to cause the skeg's mounting surface to mate with the upper gearcase. To avoid improper seating of the skeg, DO NOT FULLY TIGHTEN THESE SCREWS AT THIS POINT.
6. Replace the remaining screws. With a torque wrench, and starting with the middle screws, alternate from side to side and torque each screw progressively toward the ends of the skeg.

Torque values of skeg-to-gearcase screws are as follows:

	Ft. Lbs.	Inch Lbs.
5½ thru 50 H.P. - all model series	5-7	60-84

Marprox Sealer 1000 is the same sealer which we also recommend for sealing crankcase halves. Because it is so readily available on the wholesale and retail markets, 1000 sealer is not supplied by the factory or O.M.C.'s Parts Depot.

Figure 10-17   Installation instructions for the "spaghetti" seal that seals the joint between the two halves of the lower unit housing.

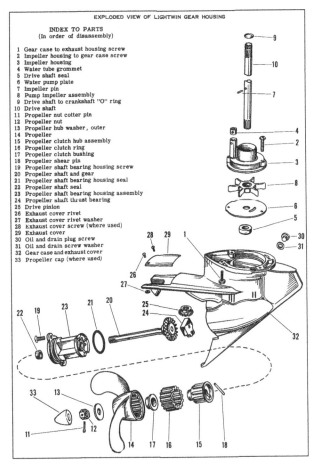

EXPLODED VIEW OF LIGHTWIN GEAR HOUSING

INDEX TO PARTS
(In order of disassembly)

1 Gear case to exhaust housing screw
2 Impeller housing to gear case screw
3 Impeller housing
4 Water tube grommet
5 Drive shaft seal
6 Water pump plate
7 Impeller pin
8 Pump impeller assembly
9 Drive shaft to crankshaft "O" ring
10 Drive shaft
11 Propeller nut cotter pin
12 Propeller nut
13 Propeller hub washer, outer
14 Propeller
15 Propeller clutch hub assembly
16 Propeller clutch ring
17 Propeller clutch bushing
18 Propeller shear pin
19 Propeller shaft bearing housing screw
20 Propeller shaft and gear
21 Propeller shaft bearing housing seal
22 Propeller shaft seal
23 Propeller shaft bearing housing assembly
24 Propeller shaft thrust bearing
25 Drive pinion
26 Exhaust cover rivet
27 Exhaust cover rivet washer
28 Exhaust cover screw (where used)
29 Exhaust cover
30 Oil and drain plug screw
31 Oil and drain screw washer
32 Gear case and exhaust cover
33 Propeller cap (where used)

Figure 10-19   Parts diagram of the non-shift "weedless" lower unit usually seen on the 3 HP models.

The final place for leaks is the "spaghetti" seal between the lower unit halves. Note the service bulletin which explains the proper installation of this seal (Figure10-17 & 10-18). After all of this, your lower unit still may leak a bit. It is difficult to get an old two-piece lower unit to seal as well as modern one-piece lower units. That is why I suggest that perfectionists lower their standards a bit when it comes to lower units.

By the way, the "non-shift" lower unit of the 3 HP models is a much simpler unit that is much easier to work on (Figure 10-19). The engine can swivel 180 degrees for reverse, and the lack of a neutral with such a small engine is not that big of a hardship, in my opinion.

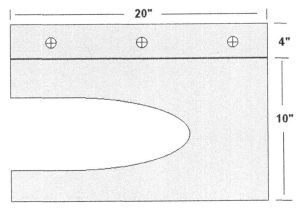

OMC Lower Unit Stand
Dimensions Approximate

Figure 10-20
Bryant Owen, a former OMC mechanic who was kind enough to review the manuscript for this book, provided this drawing of a simple fixture for holding the lower unit as you work on it. He says: "The lower unit is inserted into the gap—right side up for water pump repairs, and upside down for gearcase repairs. I used 3/4" plywood and bolted it to the edge of my workbench. The slot shown is approximate. It should be just wide enough and deep enough that the cavitation plate rests on it."   Thanks, Bryant.

Personally, I just prefer to frequently change the lower unit oil than to mess with all of the above, assuming the lower unit does not leak too badly. Only in extreme cases will I try to re-seal a lower unit. Your choice.

11

Emergency Shut-Down

Perhaps you have seen the tapes on "Funny Home Video" television shows: the riderless powerboat circling at high speed until it rams another boat or a rocky shore, as its operator, who was thrown from the boat (usually while doing something stupid) watches helplessly. Sometimes it's not so funny, as the authorities remove the body of the operator from the water after the circling boat ran him down, or even more tragically, remove the body of an innocent bystander who was run down by the uncontrolled speeding boat.

Nearly all modern outboard motors are fitted with a safety "kill-switch" which has a lanyard that the operator attaches to his person. If the operator parts company with the boat, the lanyard is pulled and the engine shuts down. This is a safety feature well worth having, and it can be easily installed on older OMC-built outboard motors. All of the engines discussed here have two cylinders and are fitted with a simple "points and condenser" ignition that is vary adaptable to lanyard safety switches. Fitting such a switch to your outboard will allow you to kill the engine before the engine can kill you. Or someone else.

The addition of a kill switch is dirt-easy if your old OMC engine was originally fitted

with a push-button shut-down switch. Have a look at Figure 11-01 which explains how the standard push-button stop-switch worked. Basically, it is just a spring-loaded switch, "normally open" (normally in the "off" position) that is connected by two wires to the ignition points. The magneto ignition system on these two-cylinder OMC engines is always "on"—in order to turn the ignition "off," an electrical connection is made between the ignition points of both cylinders. This disables both cylinders and the engine stops running. You push the stop switch, the stop switch electrically joins the two cylinder's ignition points, and the engine stops. On engines already fitted with a push-button kill switch, the existing switch can merely be replaced by the lanyard safety kill switch. If your engine was not originally fitted with the "push to stop" switch, the lanyard kill switch can still be added; it is just a little more work. You will need to run two wires for the switch up into the magneto and attach one wire to each of the ignition points (Figure 11-02).

The main item you need in order to install the safety kill switch is, of course, a kill switch (Figure 11-03). These are available through boat dealers and also through many mail-order and online marine suppliers. The important thing to remember is that you need a switch that is "normally open." Usually this type of switch is specified as a switch for magneto ignition systems, but ask questions if you are not sure. Some switches can be adapted to both "normally open" and "normally closed" applications.

Once you have your switch, you need to decide if you want to mount it to the engine,

Johnson MOTORS
November 22, 1957
Models QD-19, FD-12, RD-19C-20 Series

Service Bulletin

DEALER	✓
SERVICE MGR.	
SALES MGR.	
PARTS MGR.	
SERVICE MGR.	

Service Bulletin #606

STOP SWITCH

It will be noted that a stop switch has been included in all QD's, FD's and RD's current for 1958 to replace the familiar choke method of "stopping".

As will be observed from the schematic wiring diagram shown here, "stoppage" of ignition has been accomplished by merely shunting a lead (with switch in series) across the breaker points thus, when depressing the stop button, function of breaker point action is "voided" to "stop" sparking.

The stop switch is installed just below the control panel. In the event of remote control being desired, order assembly #377464 which is provided with terminal leads and replaces the "stop" button.

#377464 shorting switch kit

The electric starting models are equipped with a key control to replace the stop "button".

Very truly yours,

JOHNSON MOTORS

Arvid Olson
Manager - Service Promotion

MAGNETO — SCHEMATIC WIRING DIAGRAM
TO ILLUSTRATE STOP-SWITCH CIRCUIT

Shut Down is Effected by Electrically Joining the Ignition Points for Both Cylinders

Figure 11-01
Diagram shows how the factory-installed stop switch is wired; our lanyard-equipped safety kill switch will be wired in a like manner.

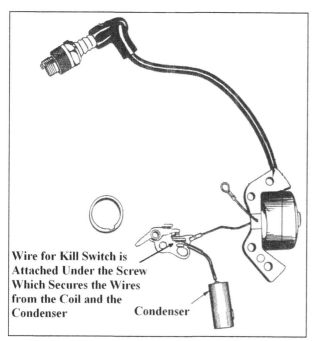

Figure 11-02
There is a single screw in the ignition points that holds both the wire from the coil and the wire from the condenser. Our kill switch wire will also be attached to this screw.

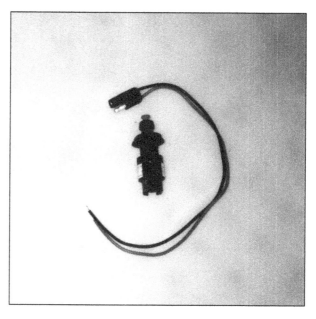

Figure 11-03
The safety kill switch, shown here without its lanyard. Also shown is a suitable style of plug for remote mounting of the safety kill switch somewhere on the boat (as opposed to somewhere on the outboard itself).

or mount it to the boat. Mounting the switch to the engine keeps you from having to run wires on the boat, and makes it very easy to transfer the engine to another boat. However, chances are you will have to fabricate some sort of bracket to mount the switch on the outboard motor, which might be more work than wiring the switch, plus the bracket may not look nice, if you are concerned about aesthetics. Finally, you really ought to purchase a spare lanyard so that if you are pitched from the boat, someone remaining in the boat can attach the spare lanyard to the motor, so it can be restarted. That way the boat can circle back to pick you up.

Mounting the switch to the boat means that one switch can serve several engines when used on that boat, each engine being fitted with a disconnect plug on the wiring. Also, in the event of

"man overboard," the disconnect plug can be disconnected, rendering the switch inoperative and allowing the engine to be restarted to go back and pick up the jetsam. However, if the connecting plug should vibrate loose or should you simply forget to plug it in, the safety switch is rendered equally inoperative.

The example installation shown here has the switch mounted in the "dashboard" of the boat (Figure 11-04). A trip to the local Radio Shack store resulted in the purchase of a low-voltage "power cord" measuring about three and a half feet in length, and featuring matching two-prong plugs at either end, and also an in-line fuse holder (Figure 11-05). Cost was about two dollars plus sales tax. You could certainly use fancier plugs, but I preferred to go cheap. The wire was cut in two, and the fuse

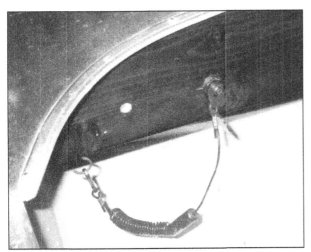

Figure 11-04
Safety kill switch mounted in the dashboard of a boat and fitted with the lanyard. The end of the lanyard hangs on a hook when the boat is not in use.

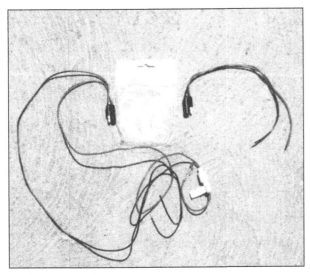

Figure 11-05
I like to use a fused low-voltage power cord that is available at a reasonable price at Radio Shack stores for installations where the safety kill switch is mounted to the boat. The cord is cut into two; one end with plug is attached to the engine while the other end and plug is incorporated into the wiring on the boat for the switch. The in-line fuse holder is removed and saved for later projects.

holder thrown in the "junk" box for use on a later project, and I now had my disconnect plugs. The example engine, a 1953 Evinrude 25 HP, did not have the existing stop switch, so I had to add the necessary wiring. The magneto was removed from the engine (see Chapter 4) and two small holes (about 1/8-inch) were drilled through the bottom of the magneto plate near the ignition points (Figure 11-06).

Be careful not to drill through anything besides the plate. Also be aware that the wires you add must not be in the way of moving parts under the plate. The plate rotates to provide "spark advance." (Figure 11-07).

The wires were then lead up through the holes and the ends were fitted with crimp-on ring terminals (Figure 11-08).

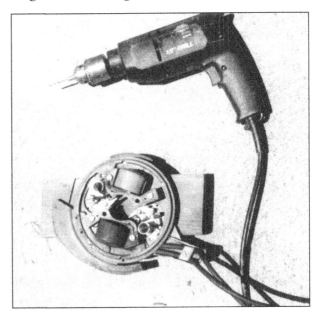

Figure 11-06
Drilling two small (about 1/8-inch) holes through the magneto plate for the kill switch wires. Keep wires clear of other components and check carefully for interference with the movement of the magneto. A small amount of electrical tape wrapped around the wire will help prevent chafing of the wire insulation.

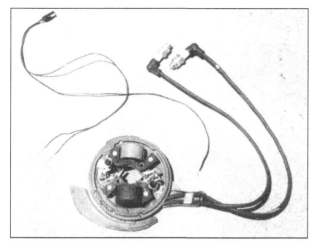

Figure 11-07
Holes drilled and wires ready to be inserted, after which ring terminals can be crimped or soldered to the wire ends for attachment under the screw heads on the ignition points.

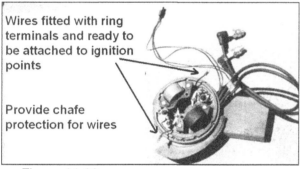

Wires fitted with ring terminals and ready to be attached to ignition points

Provide chafe protection for wires

Figure 11-08
Wires run and terminals fitted.

Then the wires were attached under the screws on each set of points—the small screws which also hold the wires from the coils and the wires from the condensers. After about twenty minutes of work, the magneto was reinstalled on the engine. Be sure to rotate the magneto through the full range of its rotation to be sure the wires will not interfere with its movement. Also be alert for possible chafe points and use padding as necessary to protect the wires. Then route the wires out of the cowling at some convenient place and the

engine is done (Figure 11-09).

The example switch was installed in a round hole drilled in the dashboard of the example boat, and then two wires lead from the switch

Figure 11-09
Wires run out through the cowl and some convenient point; a hole can be drilled and padded in order to prevent chafing, or the wires may be routed to an existing opening somewhere on the engine.

back to the transom, said wires being soldered to the wires on the other half of the Radio Shack power cord to provide the "boat end" connector plug to attach to the connector plug on the motor.

By the way, a single-cylinder engine is shut off by connecting one wire to the single set of ignition points, and the other wire to a ground on the engine.

That is all there is to it. Be sure to thoroughly test your new safety kill switch, and as mentioned before, give some thought as to how the engine can be restarted without the lanyard being present. In the case of the boat-mounted switch, give some thought to the possibility of the switch being accidentally disconnected.

12

Fuel Pump Conversion

As mentioned in Chapter 8, throughout the 1950s, most Johnson and Evinrude outboards that used remote fuel tanks were furnished with pressurized tanks which did not require a fuel pump. I am not sure why Outboard Marine Corp (OMC) continued to use the pressure tanks long after the other major manufacturer of outboards (Mercury) did away with them. Certainly a fuel pump and non-pressurized tank were a cheaper combination than the special pressure tank with its complicated priming pump and over-pressure relief valve. Indeed, the third division of OMC, the Gale division, sold lower-priced generic outboards equipped with fuel pumps, and pumps were optional equipment on some of the flagship brand Johnson and Evinrude engines.

There are a couple of issues with the pressure tanks. First, they are no longer made so only used tanks are available. Since the thin steel shells can corrode through rather quickly, it is getting harder to locate good used pressure tanks, and I have noticed that the prices are climbing, especially on the internet auction sites. (I should add that the internet auction sites are usually lousy places to buy such items, in my opinion, as the prices seem to be especially high and because you can not inspect the

tank before buying it.) Furthermore, the special quick-connect fitting that couples the fuel hose to the outboard is also a rare item that is getting hard to find. The special "twin" hose is still made but not many shops stock it.

The second issue is one of safety. The idea of carrying pressurized containers of gasoline in the boat is just plain scary to a lot of folks, especially those who smoke. Since it is very difficult to get one of these old tanks sealed completely tight it is not uncommon for them to vent small amounts of gasoline vapor. No big concern in an open boat but a very big concern in a boat with enclosed compartments. And if nothing else, a seeping pressure tank can make a real mess in the boat.

It is possible to ditch the pressure tank by converting these old OMC outboards to use a fuel pump and a standard outboard motor gasoline tank, such as those available at any boat dealer and many discount stores. For some models it is especially easy. The 10 HP and 18 HP, for example, featured a fuel pump as standard equipment after about 1960. If you can find a junker engine fitted with the fuel pump, it is a simple matter to transfer the parts to a pressure tank version (Figure 12-01). A diaphragm pump was used which utilized pressure and vacuum pulsations from the engine crankcase acting on one side of the diaphragm to pump gasoline on the other side of the diaphragm. The "transfer port" covers were the locations tapped for these pressure/ vacuum pulsations. These transfer port covers existed on most earlier pressure tank versions of the engines and were just simple castings that required little factory re-tooling in order

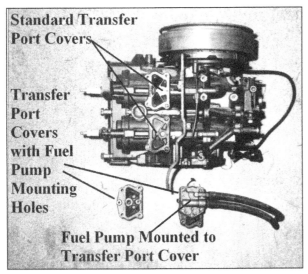

Figure 12-01
Fuel pumps were directly mounted to a transfer port cover on most OMC outboards, though not all of the outboard models had these transfer port covers, the 5½ HP being a notable exception. A port in the back of the fuel pump matched up with a hole in the transfer port cover to allow pressure/vacuum pulsations to act on the diaphragm of the pump.

Figure 12-02
Upper left is a transfer port cover intended for a direct-mounted fuel pump: note the three holes in a line and the dark-colored gasket. Lower left is a direct-mount-style fuel pump. Upper right is a transfer port fitted with a hose barb (here with a short section of old hose on it) for use with a remote-mounted fuel pump. Lower right is a pump intended for remote mounting. Only some of the larger OMC engines used remote-mounted fuel pumps. Older OMC outboards of under 20 HP that had fuel pumps used pumps that were direct mounted.

to modify them to serve as the source of the pulsations. On the models below about 20 HP, the cover was modified to have a fuel pump mounted directly to it. On models over 20 HP, the cover was either modified to have the pump mounted directly to the cover, or the cover was fitted with a hose barb and the pulsations were conducted to a remote-mounted fuel pump via a hose (Figure 12-02).

If you can locate the fuel pump, transfer port cover, and the engine-mounted quick connect fitting from a fuel-pump-equipped engine, those parts can be transferred to an earlier pressure tank version of the same engine. Once the parts are mounted, the only other task is to plug the hose barb on the intake manifold which formerly supplied the

pressure for the pressure tank. Although many people use a screw and/or epoxy for this "plugging," I will suggest that you check out your local auto parts store for little rubber nipples that are sold to hot-rodders for plugging unused vacuum lines on their modified autos. Clamping one of these nipples on the pressure barb leaves one the option of converting the engine back at some future date.

Unfortunately these conversion pieces can sometimes be difficult to locate. And some engines, such as the 7½ HP which was discontinued after 1958, never were available with the fuel pump as standard equipment. Then there is the 5½ HP which had a fuel pump after about 1960, but which never had the transfer port covers of the other models. When it was time to convert the 5½ to a standard fuel pump, OMC had to change the casting of the cylinder block to provide a mount for the fuel pump.

This chapter will show how to convert a 5½ HP OMC outboard to use a fuel pump, using "off-the-shelf" components that anybody can locate without having to frequent the outboard motor flea markets and swap meets. Although this method of conversion is the only option for converting a 5½ HP (which lacks the transfer port covers), this method will work equally well with any pressure tank OMC engine with a fuel burn that does not exceed the capacity of the pump—a little over three gallons per hour. For reference, my 1957 18 HP burns about two gallons an hour and an 18 HP or 20 HP engine would be about the biggest I would use this particular pump on. Used OEM parts to convert the larger Big Twin OMCs of 25 HP and up are much easier to find than parts for converting the smaller engines, and I would go that route if converting a Big Twin.

The pump I used on the 5.5 was a Mikuni brand rectangular or "square" pump with a single outlet, model number DF44-211 (Figure 12-03). This little pump is used on go-carts and even on some small ultra-light aircraft and is readily available through online distributors. It is a diaphragm pump operated by pressure/vacuum pulsations just like the OMC originals and is fitted with three hose barbs for attaching three hoses; one hose sup-

Figure 12-03
In the center is a the Mikuni rectangular pump used to convert the 5½ HP outboard featured in this chapter. This pump is readily available via the internet and should be suitable for outboards of up to at least 20 HP. The two motor-end quick-connect fittings on the left are the two variations of fuel-pump-style fittings used on older OMC outboards. The fitting in upper right is intended to adapt generic aftermarket fuel tanks to use OMC fuel hoses, but may also be used as a motor-end quick connector. The fitting in lower right is the motor-end quick connector used with pressure tanks.

plies fuel to the pump, a second hose conducts fuel from the pump to the carburetor, and the third hose supplies the pulsations to operate the pump. There are, of course, other pumps that will work; what is important is that the pump must be fitted with a hose barb to receive the pulsations through a hose.

As most of the OMC OEM pumps for this size of engine are arranged to bolt directly to a "port" which supplies the pulsations, they are not really suitable for this method of conversion unless you are willing to fabricate an adapter (Figure 12-04). The adapter to convert a "direct mount" pump to a "remote mount"

Threaded Hose Barb in Tapped Hole That Aligns With Port on Pump

Holes Align With Mounting Screw Holes on Pump

Figure 12-04
Diagram (not to scale) of a home-made adapter that can be used to convert a standard direct-mount OMC fuel pump to a remote-mounted fuel pump that uses a hose for pressure/vacuum pulsations. A fuel pump mounting gasket, necessary for mounting the adapter to the pump, can be used as a template when drilling the three holes. The center hole should be sized to work with 1/8" threaded hose barb (obtain barb and a tap first) while the outer holes should be about the same diameter as the fuel pump mounting holes.

pump is simply a rectangular piece of aluminum or bronze with three holes drilled in it: the center hole aligns with the port on the back of the fuel pump which receives the pressure/vacuum pulsations and this hole is threaded to receive a hose barb connector for a 1/8-inch hose (the same size hose barb as on the intake manifold.) The other two holes align with the mounting screw holes of the fuel pump. The hose barb is threaded into the center hole, and the adapter is mounted to the fuel pump using machine screws and nuts inserted into the two outside holes on the adapter and the mounting holes of the pump.

Be sure to use a standard fuel pump gasket

(OMC part number 303615 or Sierra part number 18-0850) between the pump and the adapter. The gasket can also serve as a template for laying out the holes to be drilled in the adapter. With the adapter screwed to the back of the pump, the pump can now receive its pressure/vacuum pulsations via hose. A place to mount the pump will have to be found somewhere under the cowling where there is room.

The key to making either a converted OMC pump or a Mikuni pump work in this application is to convert the source of pressure for the pressure tank into a source of pressure and vacuum to operate the pump. Pressure for the pressure tank is supplied by a hose barb located on the intake manifold, usually directly under the carburetor. The crankcases of 2-cycle engines are sealed chambers which, unlike a 4-cycle engine, are under alternating cycles of pressure and vacuum as the piston travels up and down in the cylinder. As the piston travels upwards, the crankcase is under a vacuum and the fuel/air mixture is drawn into the crankcase from the carburetor. As the piston travels downward and develops pressure in the crankcase, the fuel/air mixture is forced out of the crankcase and through the transfer ports (fitted with transfer port covers) into the combustion chamber above the piston. On a multi-cylinder engine, each cylinder's crankcase area is sealed from the other cylinders. On an "alternate firing" 2-cylinder engine, such as our subject OMC 5.5, one cylinder's crankcase will be under pressure at the same time as the other is under vacuum.

The intake manifold is fitted with passages

Figure 12-05
Carburetor has been removed. The arrow points to the hose barb on the intake manifold that supplies pressure to the pressure tank, and which after the conversion will supply pressure/vacuum pulsations to the remote-mounted fuel pump.

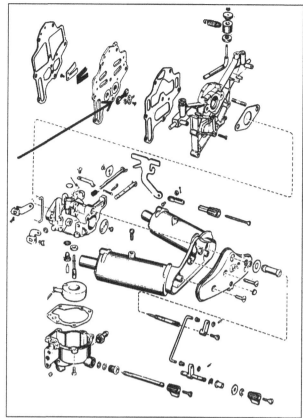

Figure 12-06
Arrow points to location of the check valves to be removed within the intake manifold assembly.

and "check valves" that permit pressure but not vacuum to be fed to the hose barb and then via hose to the pressure tank (Figure 12-05). In order for our new pump to work, we need to totally block the flow from one cylinder, and to remove the check valve from the passages from the other cylinder. That way we get both pressure and vacuum from only one cylinder (Figure 12-06). If you merely removed the check valves but did not close-off the passage from one of the two cylinders, the alternating pressure/vacuum pulsations from the two cylinders would cancel each other out.

Once these modifications have been made to the intake manifold, the rest of the conversion merely involves mounting the pump somewhere on the engine, coupling a hose from the pump to the hose barb on the intake manifold, running a hose from the pump to the quick con-

nector mounted on the engine, and finally running a hose from the pump to the carburetor.

Changing the quick-connect fitting on the engine from the pressure-tank-style connector to the fuel-pump-style will allow you to use off-the-shelf OMC fuel hoses available just about anywhere. These fuel-pump-style connectors can be purchased through any Johnson and Evinrude dealer, or you can probably locate a used fitting from a junked motor at an outboard swap meet. An alternative would be to use a fitting intended to adapt generic outboard fuel tanks to OMC fuel hoses. The fuel-pump-style OMC hose uses the same connector on both ends. Most generic gasoline tanks come with a threaded suction connection and there are OMC-style connectors available to thread into them. There is no reason one of these tank fittings could not be adapted to be the engine fitting by threading on a small pipe coupling and a hose barb. The fitting would obviously not bolt to the original mounting hole on the engine as the original equipment item would, but you could drill a hole to mount the fitting, or simply let it hang on its hose.

One final comment on the quick connector. There are a couple of different versions of the original equipment fuel-pump-style OMC quick connect motor fitting. They all fit the same fuel hose and differ only in how they mount to the motor. If you get the correct version, it will bolt right into the mounting hole vacated by the pressure tank quick connect fitting. If you end up with the wrong style fitting, you can still make it work, but you will have to make your own mounting modifications.

You will need to locate a spot "under the hood" of the engine where you can mount the fuel pump. Some of the later-style one-piece hoods have quite a bit of room available and mounting the pump will present no problems. Space is a little tight under the earlier "clamshell" style hoods, however, and you will need to be careful that the pump does not interfere with anything else such as the spark plug wires, which move as the throttle is moved. Although it would not hurt to keep the hose runs as short as possible, the pump can be mounted just about anywhere under the hood and still work properly. The pump could even be mounted on the transom of the boat as long as it is within about two feet or so of the engine.

But there would need to be three hoses running between the pump and the engine, and all three hoses would need to be disconnected in order to remove the engine from the boat.

Follow along on the parts diagram (Figure 12-07) as we begin. Remove the carburetor (#56) by removing the two nuts which hold it to the intake manifold (#43). It will probably be necessary to remove the needle valves and packing nuts (#s 39, 74, & 77) and maybe even the air silencer (#42) in order to remove the carburetor, depending upon the style of cowling that your engine has. I disconnected the carb throttle linkage at (#51) on the 1959. Set the carb aside where it won't be damaged, and remove the screws securing the intake manifold (#43). Remove the manifold and set aside. If you do not damage the gasket (#21) you can reuse it. You are now looking at the leaf plate (#30 on Figure 12-07; also Figure 12-08). Note the check valves for the pressure system (#'s 26, 27, 28, & 29, Figure 12-07); remove the leaf plate from the engine, being careful not to damage the gasket behind it, and being especially careful not to damage the reed valves and hardware mounted on the backside of the leaf plate. Remove parts #26 through #29 (Figure 12-07); you will not be using them but you should probably hang on to them in case you ever want to convert your engine back to pressure tank use.

You are now looking at gasket (#22, Figure 12-07) assuming it stayed stuck to the engine; if the gasket came off with the leaf plate, so much the better. If it is stuck to the front of the crankcase, then do not damage it by trying to

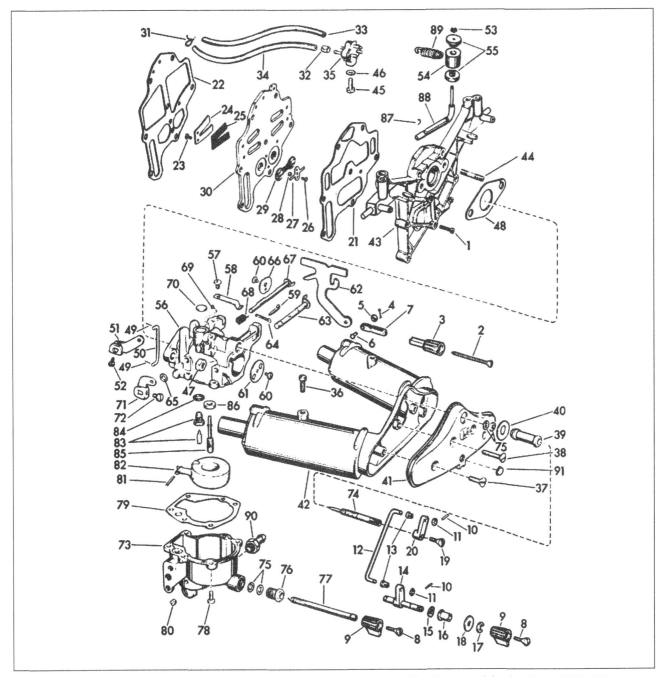

Figure 12-07   Numbered parts diagram of intake manifold assembly for the 1959 5½ HP outboard; other model outboards will be similar but not identical.

remove it. Note the curving grooves in the face of the crankcase; these are the passages that conduct pressure and vacuum from each cylinder to the check valves; we want to block off one (but *not* both) of these passages (Figure 12-09); I blocked the starboard one but it doesn't matter which one is blocked. I used an ethanol-resistant "hard-setting" gasket cement to fill the groove to seal it off. You can use something like epoxy if you wish, but if you should try to convert the engine back to the pressure tank in the future, the gasket cement would be easier to remove.

IMPORTANT NOTE: It is very important

that you not plug any passages or holes other than the one groove. Some of the passages and holes in this area of the crankcase serve to conduct the gasoline/oil mixture to bearings that require lubrication, and other passages drain excess fuel from the crankcases. Inadvertently blocking the wrong passages could result in permanent damage to your engine. Be careful not to apply excess sealant as it might get squeezed into a bad place during reassembly.

Others have made this conversion by using a large screw to plug one of the two round holes for the check valves rather than by filling one of the grooves with hard-setting gasket sealant, but to use that method risks damaging the check valve seats, greatly complicating the task of converting the engine back to pressure tank use in the future.

On the subject engine, the gasket (#22, Figure 12-07) was stuck pretty well to the face of the crankcase, so rather than risk damaging the gasket trying to remove it, I used a razor knife to cut away the gasket directly over the groove so that I could fill the groove with sealant. The sealant itself would seal the area of the gasket removed. Lastly, don't run the sealant all the way to the cylinder-end of the groove; leave just a little of the end of the groove empty to minimize the risk of the sealant ending up in the crankcase.

Once the groove of your choice is filled with sealant you can begin reassembly of the engine. Before mounting the carb, however, you might want to clamp hoses to both the fuel inlet on the carb and also the hose barb on the intake manifold, as these might be difficult to reach with the carb mounted, depending

Figure 12-08
Arrow points to check valves to be removed.

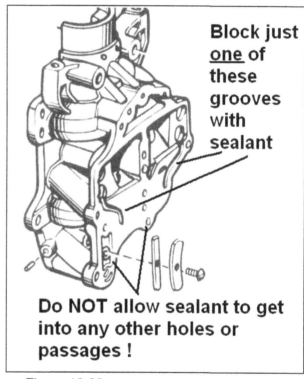

Block just one of these grooves with sealant

Do NOT allow sealant to get into any other holes or passages !

Figure 12-09
Passages to be plugged and dangers to avoid.

upon the cowl design of your particular engine. A note about hoses; I used standard automotive fuel hose, available at any auto parts store "by the foot." There is special marine fuel hose available and you might be wise to use it. Also, remember that the hose conducting the pulsations to the pump needs to withstand both pressure and vacuum so use a sturdy piece of hose.

The leaf plate and the intake manifold are screwed back onto the crankcase, and then the carb and its odds-n-ends can be installed. If the carb has not been cleaned and/or rebuilt in a while, this might be a good time to do it, with one warning: if you change several things on the engine at one time, and the darn thing won't run afterwards, it will be more difficult to trouble-shoot than if you only do one job at a time and then test-run afterwards.

With the engine back together, you need to mount the fuel pump somewhere; the cowl design of the 1959 had lots of extra room at the rear so the pump was bolted to the lower engine cover or "pan," and the hoses routed (Figure 12-10).

The fuel inlet and outlet on the pump are marked with small arrows showing the direction of fuel flow, and the hose barb for the hose from the intake manifold extends out to the side. I always incorporate a small in-line fuel filter and so installed one in the discharge hose from the pump. I like to use clear plastic filters as you can see if the filter is getting dirty and also if fuel is flowing easily.

The last part of the conversion is to change the quick connector fitting on the motor from the pressure-tank-style connector to a standard OMC fuel-pump style connector. Be sure to use clamps on all hose connections and be mindful of chafe points. By the way, there is no reason you could not use another brand of outboard fuel connector if you wanted. For example, if your little OMC engine is a back-

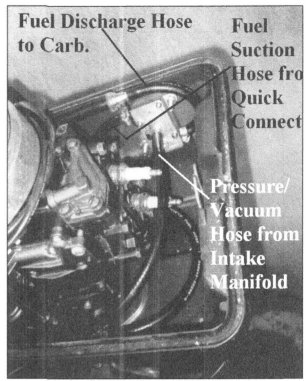

Figure 12-10
Completed fuel pump installation and hose routing: the pump may be mounted nearly anywhere there is room. Be mindful of hoses chafing or interfering with moving parts. All hose connections should be clamped and it is highly recommended that you use marine-grade hose.

up or trolling engine and your main engine is a big Mercury, you could mount a Mercury connector on the OMC engine so the same hoses and fittings could be used for both engines. Just be sure that the fuel/oil mixture is suitable for use in both engines.

That's about all there is to the conversion, other than getting a suitable remote fuel tank and hose. Considering the increasing rarity of good pressure tanks, this conversion might offer a cheaper and faster way of getting your boat underway than hunting for and repairing an old pressure tank.

Figure 12-11

A 1957 Evinrude 7½ HP converted to use a fuel pump by a reader who followed the instructions in this chapter, except using J.B Weld instead of the hard-setting gasket cement. The bent metal strap mounts are nice, except that one mount is held beneath a cylinder head bolt. I prefer to avoid disturbing head bolts if at all possible, as they sometimes have a habit of snapping off. Also, if the bolt is not properly torqued (see appendix) when tightened, the head gasket may blow out.

13

Remote Controls: Shift and Throttle

One of the many reasons that I consider these older OMC outboards to be good candidates for cheap power is that most (not all) models that were originally equipped with tiller control are readily adaptable to remote controls, and the necessary hardware is not too difficult to find or expensive. Remote control boxes and related hardware are often seen for sale at swap meets, on outboard motor online bulletin boards, and also on online auction sites. Although I generally recommend against obtaining your old outboard motor hardware on the auction sites, you can sometimes swing a good deal if you know what you are buying. One purpose of this chapter is to make you an informed buyer of remote control hardware.

If remote control is important to you, models which I would suggest avoiding are the 6 HP and 9½ HP models. These engines require some hard-to-find adapters. Unless you buy an engine that already has remote controls, you are not likely to find the parts to convert these models. I generally recommend avoiding the "low profile" engines anyway, as they are difficult to work on compared to a standard

engine. Also, as I mentioned earlier, I would avoid the "electric shift" versions of the 40 HP engines, so they will not be discussed here.

The "old-style" two-lever (short lever for shift; long lever for throttle) control box is often seen offered for sale, and will usually be the cheapest box to purchase (Figure 13-01). It

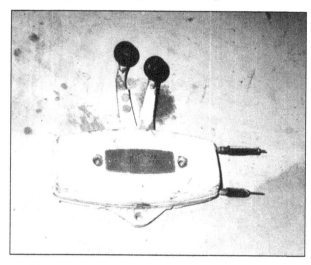

Figure 13-01
A rather beat-up remote control box from the late 1950s; identical except for paint to Evinrude and Johnson boxes, this one wears the "Bosun" label, indicating that it was originally sold with a Gale outboard motor. Note that the throttle (long) lever has been broken and repaired, and that the control cables were cut off (the ends of the cables protrude.) The cut cables are actually a good sign.

came in several colors and was fitted with labels for either Johnson or Evinrude. For the Gale division engines, such as Sea King or Sea Bee, the label read "Bosun." These boxes are all identical, except for the label and color, and will work with any of the above brands.

As research for this book, I recently purchased a complete (I will get to what I mean by "complete") Bosun control box on an online auction site for $29.99 including the shipping. I have seen similar boxes go for $50.00 to $60.00 which I consider to be high. At swap meets I will buy such boxes if they are $30.00 or less. This same style box was also available in a four lever version for twin engines. These are not often seen and usually bring a fairly high price (Figure 13-02).

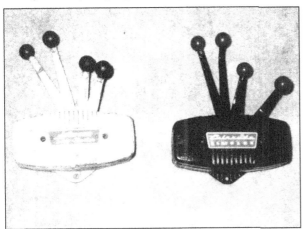

Figure 13-02
Twin-engine control boxes featured two long throttle levers and two short shift levers. Twin-engine boxes are rare; if you intend to run twins, however, you can always use two single-engine boxes.

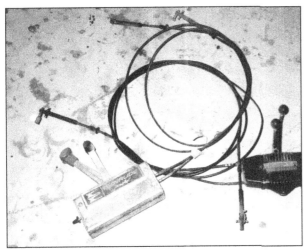

Figure 13-03
A 1960s-style square box on the left, while on the right is a 1950s-style rounded box. Note that both boxes still have their control cables attached, and that all cables still have their end fittings.

In the early-1960s the styling of the box was changed to a more squared-off look, although the boxes continued to function in a similar manner (Figure 13-03). Neither of these styles of control boxes has any provision for key-start switch, power trim, remote choke, etc. They simply control shift and throttle, and the other items, if present, where controlled from a dash panel.

If I was going to buy a box that I could not examine, such as on eBay, I would not buy one that did not still have the push-pull cables attached to it. The condition of the cables is not material; chances are they are the wrong length for your boat anyway, and new cables are readily available and dirt cheap. But you *do* want the cables present and attached to the box, because if the cables are missing, there is a good chance that part of the box is also missing. The bottoms of the levers are sector gears (a segment of a round gear) that engage a rack (flat plastic rectangle with gear teeth.) This rack is attached to the inner wire of the control cables with tiny allen-head screws which usually corrode. If whoever is removing the cables from a box does not have the proper size allen wrench, or the allen screws are corroded, there is a temptation to simply remove the cables with the racks attached. This means that part of the box has been left attached to the cables and if you only get the box, you will not have a complete box (Figure 13-04).

If you can physically examine the box, you can check for the presence of the racks. If all you have to go on is a photo, however, the presence of the cables still attached to the box is your best assurance that the racks are still in place.

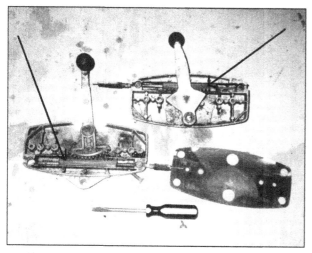

Figure 13-04
The Bosun box in Figure 13-01 opened up: Note that the racks are still present. The cutoff cables virtually guaranteed that the racks would be in place. If the cables are completely gone, there is a very good chance that the racks went with them and the box is not complete.

Another reason that you want those cables, even if they are bad, is for the fittings that attach the cables to the outboard. As I said, the cables are dirt cheap. The end-fittings are not. A control box with cables that have a bare wire on the motor-end are missing the attachment fittings. I do not consider such a box to be complete. Once adjusted, these fittings can be attached to and detached from the engine in a matter of seconds (Figures 13-05 & 13-06).

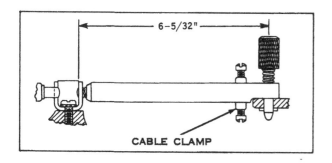

Figure 13-05
The cable end fitting for the shift cable.

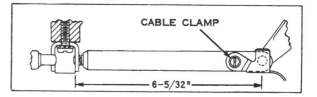

Figure 13-06
The cable end fitting for the throttle cable.

OMC used the same style control cable from the early 1950s until 1978, but outboards made after 1978 used a different style of cable. As outboards older than 1978 are the primary subject of this book, you need to be aware of this change in cables if you are in the market for used control boxes and/or cables. As for the outboard itself, all OMC outboards from 5½ HP to 40 HP (except for the electric-shift version of the 40) made from about 1955 to the early 1960s come equipped to take remote controls with a minimum of hardware. Usually all that is needed is a pair of what OMC called "locks," which were small sheet metal hooks which screwed to the cowling of the engine (Figure 13-07).

The outer sheath of the control cables is held by these locks. The cable end fittings have quick connectors to attach to the shift lever on the starboard side of the outboard, or to a throttle lever on the port side. I usually do not expect these locks to be included with a remote control box, but they are common enough at swap meets, and cheap enough to go to a dealer for if you have to. But I have often seen them already installed on engines offered for sale. Depending upon your engine model and how it is equipped, and on the type of cable lock that you can obtain, you might have to fabricate a small mounting block for

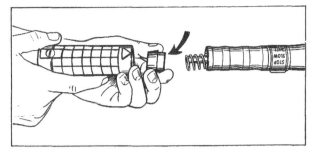

Figure 13-08
Removing the friction disc from inside the twist-grip is recommended in order to lighten the loads on the throttle cable.

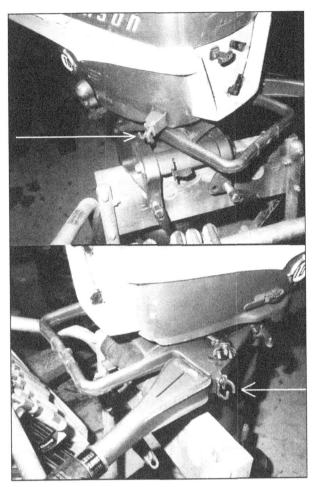

Figure 13-07
White arrows indicate the "locks" which secure the control cable sheaths.

the lock that holds the shift cable. This could be made from hardwood.

OMC recommended that the "friction disk" be removed from the twist grip to lessen the loads on the throttle control, when remote controls were installed. The twist grip can be removed by removing the single screw that retains it. Fish the disc and the disc spring out from inside the grip, and reattach the grip (Figure 13-08). There will now be much less friction on the throttle linkage. Incidentally, reattaching the grip with the disc and the spring in place can take some doing, since there are tabs and "flats" on the grip shaft

which have to be aligned. With a complete control box, new cables of the correct length for the boat (Figure 13-09), a good set of cable end fittings and cable sheath locks, you now have all you need to control the throttle and shift on a manually-started old OMC outboard (Figure 13-10 & 13-11).

But how do you kill the engine from the control station? Before they were fitted with ignition shut down switches, the engines were killed by either choking the engine or closing the throttle (retarding the throttle as far as it would go). That is how I have my 1957 Johnson 18 HP with remote controls set up on my Jim Michalak-designed 18-foot home-made cabin power skiff. If I pull the throttle all the way back, the engine dies. It works fine for me but some people can't get used to it, and want the engine to remain running at idle speed if the throttle lever is jerked back.

Starting in the late 1950s, OMC started to install an idle speed limit screw on the remote control throttle lever on the port-side of the engine. This is simply a screw which limits the travel of the throttle lever so that the engine would remain running if the lever is retarded as far as it will go. Of course, then you need

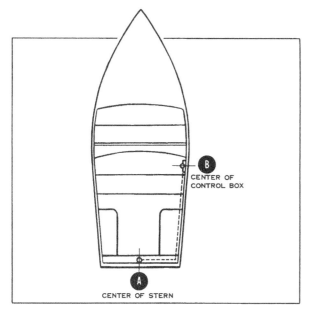

SINGLE MOTOR

DISTANCE A-B Measured along broken line	CABLE LENGTH REQUIRED (In feet)
2 to 3 feet	5
3 to 4 feet	6
4 to 5 feet	7
5 to 6 feet	8
6 to 7 feet	9
7 to 8 feet	10
8 to 9 feet	11
9 to 10 feet	12
10 to 11 feet	13
11 to 12 feet	14
12 to 13 feet	15
13 to 14 feet	16
14 to 15 feet	17
15 to 16 feet	18
16 to 17 feet	19
17 to 18 feet	20

Figure 13-09
Measuring a boat for new control cables, which may be ordered from a boat dealer or from many online sources. Note that OMC control cables from 1978 and before are different from cables for 1979 and later motors.

another way of stopping the engine.

About the same time that the idle speed limit screws started appearing, one also saw shut-down buttons start to appear on these engines (Figure 11-01). All the engines we are talking about here are two-cylinder, with a set

of breaker points for each cylinder. The shut-down button had a wire connected to each of the two sets of points, and when the button was pushed, the two wires were connected together, which shorted-out both sets of points and shut the engine down. It would be a simple matter to extend these two wires up to the remote control location and install a switch of your choice- spring-loaded momentary contact (such as a horn button), toggle switch, or even key switch. Just keep in mind that, with these magneto ignition systems, when the switch is "open" the ignition is on, and when the switch is closed, the ignition is off. If your engine did not come with the shut-down button, you can still wire a remote shutdown by running two wires from the breaker points on the magneto in the same manner as the safety kill switch is installed (see Chapter 11), to a normally-open switch at the helm position. For that matter, it would not be a bad idea to wire-in a safety "kill switch" with a lanyard at the remote control location so that if you are thrown from the boat, the engine will shut down.

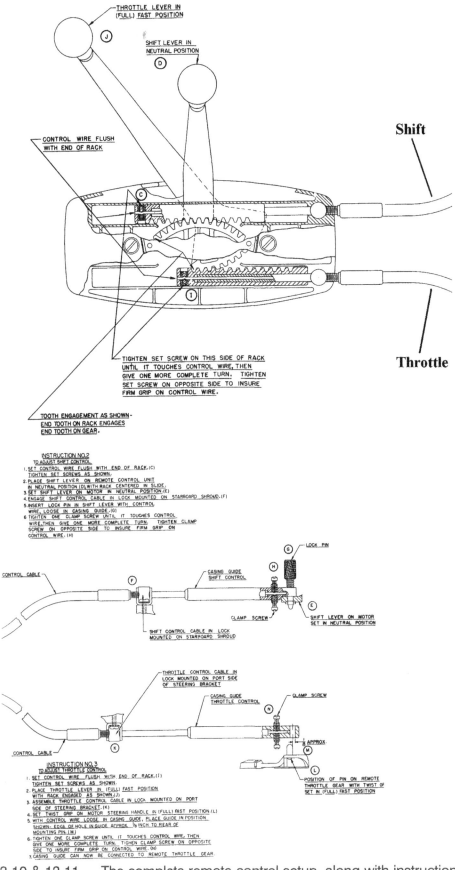

Shift

Throttle

THROTTLE LEVER IN
(FULL) FAST POSITION

SHIFT LEVER IN
NEUTRAL POSITION

CONTROL WIRE FLUSH
WITH END OF RACK

TIGHTEN SET SCREW ON THIS SIDE OF RACK
UNTIL IT TOUCHES CONTROL WIRE, THEN
GIVE ONE MORE COMPLETE TURN. TIGHTEN
SET SCREW ON OPPOSITE SIDE TO INSURE
FIRM GRIP ON CONTROL WIRE.

TOOTH ENGAGEMENT AS SHOWN-
END TOOTH ON RACK ENGAGES
END TOOTH ON GEAR.

INSTRUCTION NO.2
TO ADJUST SHIFT CONTROL.
1. SET CONTROL WIRE FLUSH WITH END OF RACK.(C)
   TIGHTEN SET SCREWS AS SHOWN.
2. PLACE SHIFT LEVER ON REMOTE CONTROL UNIT
   IN NEUTRAL POSITION (D), WITH RACK CENTERED IN SLIDE.
3. SET SHIFT LEVER ON MOTOR IN NEUTRAL POSITION.(E)
4. ENGAGE SHIFT CONTROL CABLE IN LOCK MOUNTED ON STARBOARD SHROUD.(F)
5. INSERT LOCK PIN IN SHIFT LEVER WITH CONTROL
   WIRE, LOOSE IN CASING GUIDE.(G)
6. TIGHTEN ONE CLAMP SCREW UNTIL IT TOUCHES CONTROL
   WIRE, THEN GIVE ONE MORE COMPLETE TURN. TIGHTEN CLAMP
   SCREW ON OPPOSITE SIDE TO INSURE FIRM GRIP ON
   CONTROL WIRE. (H)

LOCK PIN

CONTROL CABLE

CASING GUIDE
SHIFT CONTROL

SHIFT LEVER ON MOTOR
SET IN NEUTRAL POSITION

CLAMP SCREW

SHIFT CONTROL CABLE IN LOCK
MOUNTED ON STARBOARD SHROUD

THROTTLE CONTROL CABLE IN
LOCK MOUNTED ON PORT SIDE
OF STEERING BRACKET

CASING GUIDE
THROTTLE CONTROL

CLAMP SCREW

APPROX.

CONTROL CABLE

POSITION OF PIN ON REMOTE
THROTTLE GEAR WITH TWIST OF
SET IN (FULL) FAST POSITION

INSTRUCTION NO.3
TO ADJUST THROTTLE CONTROL
1. SET CONTROL WIRE FLUSH WITH END OF RACK.(I)
   TIGHTEN SET SCREWS AS SHOWN.
2. PLACE THROTTLE LEVER IN (FULL) FAST POSITION
   WITH RACK ENGAGED AS SHOWN.(J)
3. ASSEMBLE THROTTLE CONTROL CABLE IN LOCK MOUNTED ON PORT
   SIDE OF STEERING BRACKET.(K)
4. SET TWIST GRIP ON MOTOR STEERING HANDLE IN (FULL) FAST POSITION.(L)
5. WITH CONTROL WIRE LOOSE IN CASING GUIDE, PLACE GUIDE IN POSITION
   SHOWN- EDGE OF HOLE IN GUIDE APPROX. 1/8 INCH TO REAR OF
   MOUNTING PIN. (M)
6. TIGHTEN ONE CLAMP SCREW UNTIL IT TOUCHES CONTROL WIRE, THEN
   GIVE ONE MORE COMPLETE TURN. TIGHTEN CLAMP SCREW ON OPPOSITE
   SIDE TO INSURE FIRM GRIP ON CONTROL WIRE. (N)
7. CASING GUIDE CAN NOW BE CONNECTED TO REMOTE THROTTLE GEAR.

Figures 13-10 & 13-11   The complete remote control setup, along with instructions for installing end fittings on cables, installing cables into control boxes, and adjusting the link.

14

Remote Controls: Steering

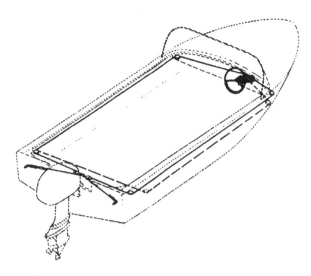

Figure 14-02
Diagram of the general layout of the cables of a cable-over-sheave (pulley) steering system. Note that the runs of the cable from the steering wheel can be lead down just one side of the boat or down both sides of the boat, as required by the design of the boat. Side-console boats usually need both cables run down one side, for example.

It does little good to control shift, throttle, and shut-down from a remote location unless you can also control steering. Before we delve into remote steering, however, we should consider an alternative: the tiller extension. For a smaller boat that can be controlled from the general vicinity of the motor, a tiller extension makes a lot of sense. There were factory-made tiller extensions for these old OMC engines (Figure 14-01), but one can be easily made from PVC pipe. Keep in mind that it needs to be strong and reliable—if it fails, injury or death could result.

But if you just *have* to have a steering wheel. . . . Back in the 1950s and early 1960s, the

Figure 14-01
Two factory-made tiller extensions. A tiller extension (either factory-made or home-made) may provide all of the "remote control" you need at a bargain price.

most common outboard remote steering system by far was the cable-over-sheave (pulley) system (Figure 14-02). The components for these systems were readily available and cheap, and despite what boat dealers say about them, they were safe and reliable and very fixable by your average Joe. The only reason that they fell out of favor was because they can be time-consuming to install compared to push-pull cable and hydraulic systems. Don't you believe it when a boat dealer or mechanic tells you that such systems are suitable only for low-horsepower engines. I have personally piloted commercial vessels a hundred feet long equipped with cable-over-sheave steering. As long as the system is laid out correctly and the hardware properly sized to the job, these systems can be reliable and relatively friction free. And anyway, we *are* talking about low-horsepower engines here.

I would very much recommend that before you try to install one of these cable-over-pulley steering systems, you have a close look at a boat that has one. A friend or maybe a used boat dealer might have one of these that you can examine. Note the placement of the sheaves and fairleads, and how obstructions are dealt with.

To install a cable-over-sheave steering system you first need a helm unit, or steerer, consisting of a cable drum, steering wheel, and the stuff that holds them together and mounts them. Other than expensive racing units, these cable-drum helm units are no longer manufactured. But used units are often seen at swap meets and online auction sites. There are several different variations; some have the drum mounted on the exterior of the dashboard; some have the drum mounted on the interior of the dashboard, and the shaft to the steering wheel either runs through the dash, or under the dash. The cheapest and easiest units to find will have an automotive-style steering wheel and the drum on the inside of the dash (Figure 14-03). The outboard racers and antique outboard motor collectors tend to drive up the prices of external drum helm units with automotive wheels (Figure 14-04), and the nautical collectors drive up the prices of anything with a ship's wheel (Figure 14-05).

Also, note that the steering shaft may mount perpendicular to the dash panel or at an angle to the dash panel. Being flexible should get you a reasonably priced helm unit.

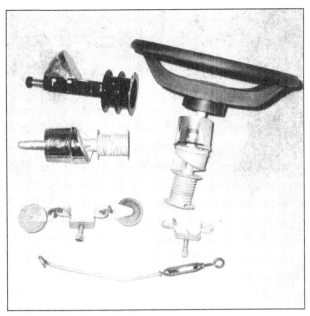

Figure 14-03
On the right is a complete "internal drum" (drum behind the dashboard) helm or steering unit. Top left is an internal drum unit (without steering wheel) that runs the steering shaft under the dashboard; below that is an internal drum unit that runs the shaft through the dashboard. Also note that the bezels of all three of the helm units place the steering wheel at an angle to the dashboard. Also shown are two steering attachment fittings (See Figure 14-06) for attaching the steering cables to an OMC outboard. One of these fittings has its two sheaves fitted. Also shown is a twin-engine tie bar.

Although newer units have a shaft with a standard taper that will accept most modern marine steering wheels, be advised that some really old helm units from the 1950s and maybe early 1960s might have an odd shaft arrangement, so you had better get a steering wheel with the helm unit.

The other parts needed are sheaves, cable, and maybe fairleads (which are used where the steering cable needs to make a slight bend), and some way to attach the cable to the out-

Figure 14-04
Two external drum steering units. These usually sell for a higher price and are harder to find than the internal drum units. Also shown are two "deadman" racing throttles, which are spring-loaded to shut down the motor if the driver releases his grip (as in the event of being thrown overboard!)

Figure 14-05
External drum helm units fitted with "ship's wheels." These are always expensive due to interest from collectors.

board. Nearly all (but not all) of the OMC outboards that we are talking about feature a steering-attachment mounting hole in the "carry handle" on the front of the engine. With a genuine OMC steering attachment (Figure 14-06), hooking the steering up to an engine is a one-minute job once you have

rigged all of the cables and sheaves. If one lacks the proper attachment it is possible to engineer something that will work.

Which brings us again to safety. If your steering system fails, someone could get hurt or killed. This means that you should use lock-nuts or thread locking compound on all bolted connections. It is always preferable to through-bolt sheaves rather than fastening them with screws (Figure 14-07). It also means that you must thoroughly test your steering system before putting it into service, and that you inspect it regularly. Laying out the cable runs is the hard part. It will take a little time, and you will run into problems, but they can be solved. For instance, if you are running your steering cables along the insides of the hull, but the hull sides curve fore and aft, the cable, which is under tension and straight, is six inches or more away from the curving side of the boat amidships. No problem. Just install a few fairleads to hold the cable in close to the hull sides (Figure 14-09). The slight amount of drag that the fairleads will induce will not be a problem. If, however, you need to make a corner of about 20 degrees or more, you had better use a sheave.

When I installed cable-over-sheave steering in my home-made power skiff, I mounted the wheel to starboard on the aft bulkhead of the cabin and ran both cables down the starboard side of the boat with a couple of fairleads to hold them close to the curving side of the hull. After both cables pass through holes in the forward motor well bulkhead, one cable turns 90 degrees over a sheave and leads to the port side of the boat (Figure 14-08). Two more sheaves

EVINRUDE
SERVICE BULLETIN

Service Department
EVINRUDE MOTORS
Milwaukee 16, Wisconsin

MISCELLANEOUS
NUMBER M-78

October 18, 1954

SIMPLEX REMOTE CONTROL

The 1955 Evinrude Big Twin introduces a reverse method of connecting the Tiller Attachment Part #376018. This change places the Tiller Attachment between the steering bracket and the motor, protecting it while the motor is being tilted forward.

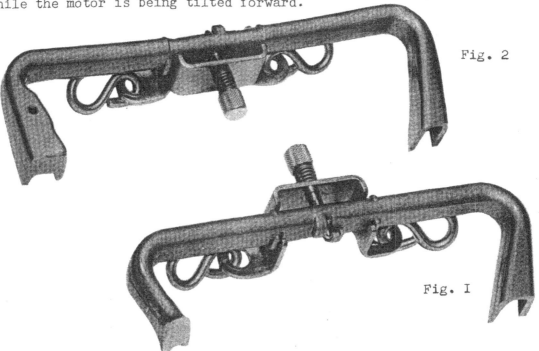

Fig. 2

Fig. I

The Tiller Attachment is not changed in design but is installed in reverse position.

Note two small lugs cast on the steering bracket. The lock screw reaches thru the bracket and the pin in the end of the lock screw anchors against these lugs.

The above paragraph will guide you to the proper installation in either case.

Figure 1 explains the lug location used in the past and on the 1955 Fleetwin and Fastwin. Note the lug location is on the inside of the bracket. The proper position of the Tiller Attachment is shown.

Figure 2 explains the outside lug position on the bracket as found on the 1955 model Big Twin and the proper position of the Tiller Attachment.

Use the lug location on the bracket as your guide.

Figure 14-06   Fitting for attaching the steering cables to the "carry" handle found on the front of nearly every OMC outboard made from about 1951 until the early '70s. These fittings are common items at outboard motor swap meets and can be found used via the internet. It is also possible to install an eye bolt in the carry handle for the cable attachment, but be sure to thoroughly test any "home-brew" engineering in the interest of safety.

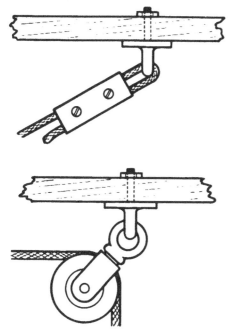

Figure 14-07
All fittings should be through-bolted with the possible exception of fairleads that do not radically change the direction of a cable.

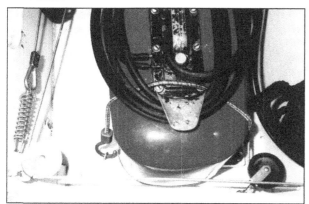

Figure 14-08   You are looking at the motor well; the bow is to the right, the transom to the left, and the outboard is above. Both steering cables run down the starboard side of the boat (bottom of photo). The black pulley to the right redirects one cable over to the port side of the boat so that, after passing through two more sheaves, the cable can be lead to the port side of the motor. The white sheave to the left leads its cable to the starboard side of the motor. The fuel tank is chocked and strapped down so that it can not move and bind the steering cables.

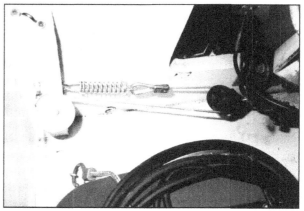

Figure 14-09
Transom is to the top of the photo; motor to the right; The cable leading to the starboard side of the motor is visible. The cable passes from the sheave at the corner of the transom and leads to the sheave on the motor attachment fitting, then returns to the corner of the transom where the end of the cable is secured to a spring as shown in Figure 14-10. It would not hurt to use two clamps on the end of the cable, instead of just the one shown.

lead it to the port side of the motor. The remaining cable stays to starboard and turns to meet the motor with one sheave mounted in the starboard stern corner of the motor well (figure 14-09). If you intend to have a side console, you will probably have to run each cable down one side of the boat as well.

It is common practice to lead the cables to a sheave on the motor connector and then return it to the corners of the boat. Here they are secured to compression springs to allow for changing cable length when the motor is tilted up (Figure 14-10). This gives a 2-to-1 mechanical advantage to the steering system which is all the "power steering" that you get or need.

It is important to have the anchor points for the final sheave at the transom, and the end of the cable, as closely aligned as possible with the axis of the outboard motor tilt "hinge pin" or tilt tube. This will minimize the tendency of the cables to go slack or tighten as the motor is tilted up or down.

Once you hassle with laying out these cables, sheaves, and fairleads, you will see why boat builders and dealers prefer to install push-pull cables. But if you lay it out right and don't have the cable dragging on anything, you will have a very friction-free steering system at less cost than the more common push-pull cable systems.

Alternatively, you can buy a brand-new push-pull system and figure out how to adapt it to your old engine. I have adapted these new systems to old outboards, but you have to engineer your own connector kits. Plus, the cable and sheave system can be very cheap if you run into a deal, such as someone removing a whole system to replace it with something more modern. Often the old system will be offered for sale, complete and cheap.

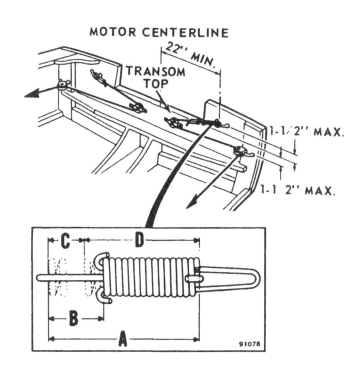

Figure 14-10
Diagram showing the recommended arrangement of sheaves and springs at the transom. Note that this gives a 2-to-1 mechanical advantage to the steering system, giving the helmsman more leverage at the steering wheel, but requiring more turns of the wheel to go from "lock to lock" (wheel turned all the way one way to wheel turned all the way the other way).

15

Big Twin Tiller Conversion

Virtually all OMC engines of under 25 HP (and also some very early 1970s 25s) came from the factory fitted with a tiller, so no additional parts or work is required for tiller control of these engines. Unless a previous owner has removed the tiller when one of these engines was fitted with remote controls (OMC recommended leaving the tiller in place), you will get the tiller with the engine. "Big Twins," however, were available either with a tiller or without a tiller (for remote control only). So if you want tiller control over one of the latter engines, a tiller must be mounted.

Converting a non-tiller Big Twin to tiller control is no big deal (Figure 15-01). These remote-control engines usually came fitted with an engine-mounted "flipper-handle" throttle mounted on the forward port side of the engine (Figure 15-02). Sometimes this was referred to as a warm-up throttle, for use when starting the engine from the engine, rather than from the remote control location. To install a tiller the warm-up throttle is simply removed from the engine, and a tiller bolted on in its place.

But first, you must acquire a Big Twin tiller. These are common swap meet items, and also are sometimes seen on the online auction sites. Lastly, one can often be purchased through a dealer of used outboard parts. I consider a reasonable price for a complete Big Twin tiller to be $30.00 to $50.00. However, the more convenient it is to obtain, the more expensive it will most likely be, and I have heard of price quotes of $100.00 from the used parts resellers.

Here are a couple things to keep in mind: First of all, make sure you are buying a Big Twin tiller and not a tiller from another model. The only other style of twist-grip throttle tiller used on OMC engines made during the time period in question is much shorter than a Big Twin tiller, and the Big Twin tiller bolts to the engine differently (Figure 15-03). Also, the interior throttle shaft is visible from the underside of a Big Twin tiller, but is totally enclosed within the tiller housing of the other OMC tillers (Figure 15-04).

Also, be advised that two different styles of cogs were used in Big Twin tillers. Twist-grip throttle tillers used on all OMC engines from this period all work in the same manner: the rotating twist-grip throttle is coupled to an internal shaft in the tiller itself. This shaft has to have a flexible coupling at the hinge point of the tiller (where the tiller folds upward). This flexible coupling is accomplished by interlocking "cogs" on the tiller's shaft, and also on the throttle shaft extending into the motor. I refer to the two different styles of cogs used, as pointy-toothed cogs (used up until 1956) and ball-tooth cogs (used after 1956). It really does not matter which style cog you use.

Evinrude
Service Bulletin

Service Department
EVINRUDE MOTORS
Milwaukee 16, Wisconsin

BIG TWIN
NUMBER 25.-55
May 2, 1955

INSTALLATION, STEERING HANDLE, BIG TWIN

To minimize the possibility of breakage in shipment Big Twin motors in the future will be packed with the steering handle removed. The handle will be packed separately in the motor carton.

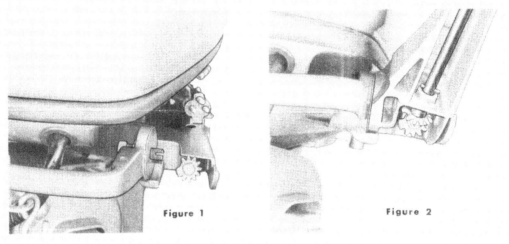

Figure 1   Figure 2

Instructions covering the proper method of installing the steering handle are described and illustrated.

1. Remove the cotter pin and nut from the hinge bolt.

2. Rotate the front gear in the handle bracket until the wide tooth space, faces the hinge bolt. Figure 1.

3. Move the steering handle into position as shown in Figure 2, making sure the metal friction washer is between the handle and steering bracket.

4. Before meshing the gears, rotate the twist grip until the large gear tooth (handle) aligns with the large tooth space in the handle bracket gear. Push the gears into mesh.

5. Turn the hinge bolt until it extends through the handle approximately 1/16 inch.

6. Tilt the handle upward and add the nut. Tighten the bolt and nut. Be sure the gears remain in mesh during this phase of assembly. See Figure 2.

7. The handle can now be lowered and tried for proper operation. Do not force the handle, to lower it or to turn the twist grip as the gears can easily be damaged if they are not properly meshed.

8. When the assembly functions properly, raise the handle, tighten the bolt to obtain the desired hinge friction, then tighten the nut and secure it with a cotter pin.

EVINRUDE MOTORS

H. Dickerson

Figure 15-01   Installing a tiller on a Big Twin is no big deal with the right pieces, but before the tiller can be attached, a few other parts need to be removed.

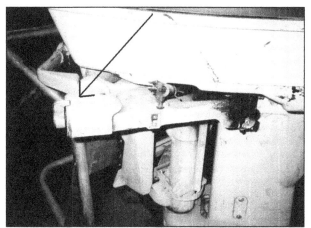

Figure 15-02
Arrow points to the "flipper handle" or warm-up throttle control that will be removed and replaced with the tiller.

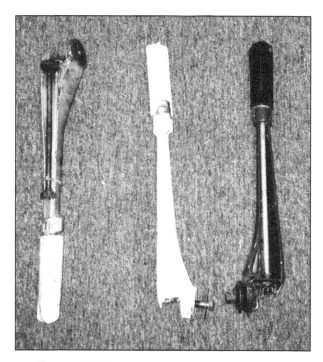

Figure 15-04
Three Big Twin tillers of the kind that you do want; the one on the left has the additional shaft taped to it (so the shaft does not get lost); way over to the right is the shaft that you need to get with the tiller. Note that the underside of the tiller is hollow and you can see the inner shaft.

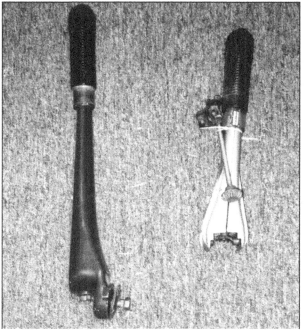

Figure 15-03
On the left is the tiller you want; on the right is a tiller that you do not want. Note the differences.

They are interchangeable, but you *do* need to have two of the same style cog. Also, the ball-tooth cog will be seen to have one extra-large tooth and one extra-large gap. In other words, they can engage in only one relative position. Attempting to force engagement with one cog rotated out of alignment may damage these cogs.

I mentioned the throttle shaft extending into the engine. A complete tiller will include this shaft, which should come with the cog needed to engage the cog on the tiller (Figure 15-05). The other end (aft end) of the throttle shaft may or may not come fitted with the pinion gear that engages the vertical throttle shaft. This gear is already on the engine and it is not necessary to get that piece as well. You do need to get the shaft, though, as the "flipper handle" is permanently attached to the shaft already in a "remote control-only" Big Twin, and it cannot be used with the tiller.

Finally, you should try to get the attaching hardware for the tiller, which will consist of a bolt and nut, a dished-and-notched lock

159

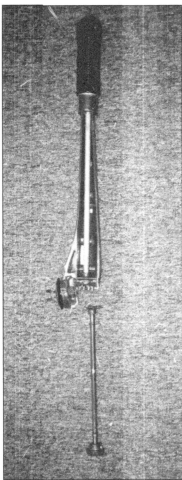

Figure 15-05
A Big Twin tiller and also the shaft that you should get when you buy or trade for a tiller.

Figure 15-06
White arrow points to a wrench on the mounting bolt for the cowl or cover over the warm-up, or flipper throttle. Some of these bolts are reached from above, as here, and some from underneath.

washer, and a very thin friction washer.

Step one to making the conversion is to degrease the engine so you can see what you are working on. I degreased the example engine in 10 degree F weather where the water was freezing on the engine and on me. (Such was my dedication to this book.) Next, remove the large bolt that holds the throttle cover or cowling on. The cover itself cannot be removed until the flipper handle and shaft are removed, but get the cover loose anyway. Note that in the photo (Figure 15-06), the big bolt is accessed from above; on some engines you

need to go in from underneath to get to the bolt. Next, remove the small set-screw from the pinion gear at the aft end of the throttle shaft on the motor proper (Figure 15-07). Remove this screw entirely, as it passes through a notch in the shaft, and loosening it only—as it appears would work—will not work. (Guess who, having not made this conversion for several years, forgot about that when trying to remove the gear from the shaft for these photos?)

Next, have a look at the shaft from underneath (Figure 15-08). Some of these engines will have a stop mounted on the shaft that limits its maximum rotation. This is what keeps the engine from idling too slow by limiting how far the throttle can be retarded. This stop, which looks like a small lever, will be pinned to the shaft and will need to be removed in order to remove the shaft. Not all engines have this stop. Use a hammer and very small punch to

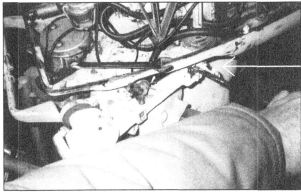

Figure 15-07
Removing the pinion gear from the warm-up throttle shaft so that the shaft can be removed and be exchanged for the tiller handle throttle shaft. Note parka: Brrrrr!

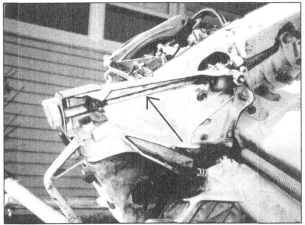

Figure 15-08   Black arrow points to where you might find a small lever which acts as a throttle stop to prevent the throttle from being retarded so much that the engine dies. A threaded screw provides adjustment for the stop. This engine does not have it, but if your engine does, and you remove the stop and don't reinstall it on the new throttle shaft, the engine will die if you retard the throttle all the way.

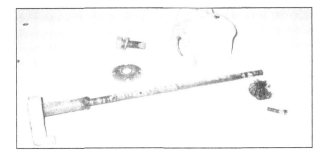

Figure 15-09
The parts that are removed from the outboard; the warm-up or flipper throttle shaft and its pinion gear and pinion gear screw; the cover or cowl, and the bolt and notched washer that will be used to bolt the tiller handle on.

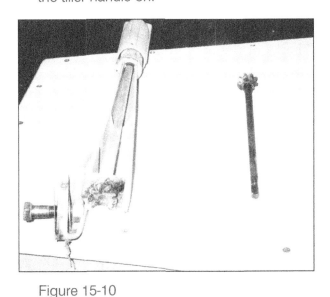

Figure 15-10
The tiller handle and its throttle shaft; note the large gap in the teeth at the bottom of the cog. This gap will accept one oversized tooth in the cog on the upper end of the throttle shaft. These are the ball-tooth style cogs.

remove the roll pin which holds the stop on. You can now withdraw the shaft from the engine. The pinion gear will be loose, so watch that it does not get lost. Also, there may be small plastic bushings that support the shaft where it passes through the webs of the castings. Don't lose them (Figure 15-09).

You are halfway done. Insert the throttle shaft for the tiller into the engine and attach the pinion gear to its aft end (Figure 15-10). Note that the shaft and the gear have a "flat" on them for alignment. Try rotating the throttle shaft back and forth to be sure that neither the pinion gear nor the gear on the vertical throttle shaft "run out of teeth" at the extreme limits of rotation. Then you simply bolt the tiller on, being sure to line up the cogs correctly. The very thin washer goes between the tiller and its mounting boss. Also note that a nut is used on the mounting bolt. A nut was not used on the cover that was originally there.

I wish to emphasize that the tiller controls both the throttle and the steering of your engine, so make sure the lock washer is used on the mounting bolt, and a bit of liquid thread-locking compound such as Locktite would not be a bad idea either. Frequent checks of the mounting hardware during the first few hours of operation are also warranted. Make sure that the throttle mechanism operates smoothly. The most common problem that I have seen is for bushing wear on the throttle shafts to allow the hinge-point cogs to sometimes "skip" or "jump" teeth. Although the proper fix is to replace the little plastic bushings through which the shafts pass, I have on occasion managed a reliable fix by adding a shim between the cogs and the webs of the castings (through which the shaft passes) by inserting either a very thin washer or sometimes even a twist of copper wire. If you try shimming, however, be careful that you don't shim too much, or the tiller may not "hinge down" all the way. (Figure 15-11).

You will probably want more steering friction with a tiller than was used with remote steering. These engines are fitted with steering friction screws in different locations. However, as I feel the friction available to be inadequate, I have often run these engines with bungee cords running from the engine to each side of

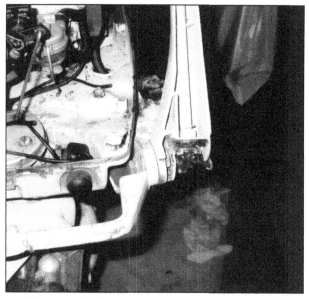

Figure 15-11
The tiller bolted into place and raised to its upright position; cog engagement must be tight enough so that the cogs will not "jump teeth," but not so tight that the tiller will not lower fully to the "down" position. Shimming might be necessary to achieve both goals, and badly worn cogs might need replaced.

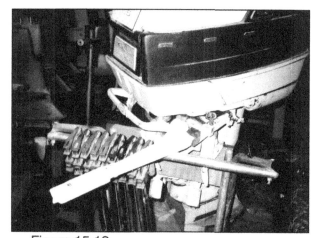

Figure 15-12
Completed tiller installation. Make SURE that the tiller mounting bolt can not loosen, and that the full range of throttle movement is available before heading out on the water.

the boat, such that the engine will self-center if the tiller is released. It is also possible to fit these engines with lanyard shut-offs similar to modern outboards, and I would highly recommend that you install such a switch on your engine. (See Chapter 11.)

Removing the necessary hardware and mounting the tiller should take you no more than an hour or two, and the tiller can also be used in conjunction with remote controls, giving you "two-station" control of your boat. Just keep in mind that a control failure could cause injury (or worse) to you or someone else. So be sure the tiller is securely mounted and that the throttle function works smoothly, and as mentioned, a lanyard safety shut-down is also not a bad idea.

Figure 15-13
They say a boy never forgets his "first." Tiller conversion, that is. I converted this 1959 Evinrude 35 HP to tiller control back in 1995 and used it all one summer on the Mississippi, then hung it on a rack and have not used it since. Still have it.

16

Trouble-shooting

Most outboard motor service manuals have a section on "trouble-shooting," or diagnosing of what ails an outboard. I will include my own thoughts on the matter here. What I am going to emphasize, however, is not a list of specifics but rather an attitude.

You see 'em all the time at the launch ramp: a guy sitting in boat (usually blocking the ramp as others wait impatiently to launch or retrieve their boats), either yanking his guts out pulling on the starting rope, or endlessly grinding on the electric starter (until the battery is dead). But the darn outboard motor just will not start. This is not the place to learn that your motor does not run, at least not on a crowded launch ramp on a busy weekend. With others waiting to occupy the spot that you are using, there is simply too much pressure and too little time to properly diagnose the problem. All you are going to accomplish in such a situation is to work yourself into a frenzy of frustration that is not likely to make you popular with other family members.

The first step to prevent such situations is what I refer to as "bucket cruising." This is simply running the outboard in a bucket of water to be sure it runs before you head to the launch ramp (Figure 16-01). I do this at the

Figure 16-01
The 1955 Johnson 5½ HP that serves as an auxiliary motor for my 18-foot Jim Michalak-designed cabin skiff gets its springtime test run in the 55-gallon plastic barrel.

beginning of the boating season and also after performing any repairs or maintenance on an engine. Now, just because it runs in a bucket of water does not mean that it will run properly with the boat in the water, but at least you can be reasonably sure it will start. Long ago (1979) and far away (Table Rock Lake in Southwest Missouri), I once launched my then ten-year-old boat with an 85 HP outboard on a cold and windy fall day. I had just picked up the boat from having some work done on the upholstery and was anxious to get in one last day on the water before winterizing it. As the ramp had no dock, I backed the trailer down into the water, pushed the boat off the trailer and hopped aboard to start the engine and motor around to where I could beach the boat and then park the truck and trailer. The short of a long story: the battery was dead, the outboard would not start, the wind was pushing me out into the middle of Table Rock Lake, and as it was a cold and windy fall day, few other boats were around. Luckily, another boat happened along after I had drifted a bit, and towed me back close to the trailer, where I was able to jump into waist-deep water and get the boat back on the trailer. At some point the ignition key had been left in the "on" position, probably because I had run the gasoline out of the motor at the end of the previous boating trip and forgot to turn the key "off" after the motor quit. A test-run in a bucket of water or with a flush attachment would have identified that problem before it left me drifting across the lake.

I sometimes just hang out at ramps as a form of personal entertainment; you never know just what you will see. Once I witnessed a Ford pickup get "launched." Some people I have observed at the boat ramp seem to think an abbreviated form of bucket cruising: the test-starting of the outboard while the boat is still out of the water ("ramp cruising"?) It is not a good idea, as detailed in Figure 06-15. And anyway, running the outboard only a few seconds, while perfectly capable of damaging your outboard, is not enough to tell you if it is overheating or if the motor is simply running on gasoline contained in the carburetor and not receiving fuel from the fuel tank.

Figure 16-02
Next is the 1957 Johnson 18 HP which serves as the main engine: I have owned this particular engine for over ten years, have used it on several different boats, and it has never let me down. I keep it maintained, replace the pump impeller and other "wear" items every few years, and test-run it at the beginning of every boating season.

I usually use a 55-gallon plastic drum with the top cut off for my bucket cruising (Figure 16-02). But a good-sized garbage can will serve if is watertight (mine usually aren't). Leave the motor clamped to your boat, back the trailer up to the drum/garbage can, and tilt the motor down into the water. Be sure that the water pump at the top of the lower unit is submerged, and be sure that the trailer can't move (block the wheels or leave it coupled to your tow vehicle). Start the outboard up and let it run for five minutes or so, to ensure that it is pumping cooling water and pumping fuel. There should be cooling water discharging from somewhere at the rear of the engine below the power head. The exact place varies from model to model, but it is usually a water spray emanating from an exhaust relief outlet. The water spray should be warm after a few minutes running, but not so hot that you can't keep your hand in it. Keep in mind that the exhaust gas is also hot. You might try shifting the engine into gear but be prepared for a tsunami if you speed the engine up beyond idle. Also be mindful that the propeller can eat your garbage can.

I generally leave my drum full of water year round, an option you do not have if you need to use your garbage can for the garbage. Before dumping the water, notice that even a few minutes of running has left a thin layer of oil/sludge/gasoline on top of the water (Figure 16-03). It's not quite as bad as it looks, as a very small amount of these items can cover a lot of water surface area, but it is still pollution, and it is the reason that many environmentalists don't like old 2-cycle outboard motors. Although I am not a hard-core "tree-hugger" (a term I use with the respect due to anyone making an effort to protect our planet from ourselves), I understand the need to minimize the scars we leave upon this earth. I leave my drum full of water rather than frequently dumping it and when the sludge gets thick I skim it off (an old swimming pool skimming

Figure 16-03
Yuk. Oily scum left after test-running old outboards. If you dump this stuff onto the ground or down the sewer then you are part of the problem; be part of the solution and soak this stuff up with absorbent pads made for the purpose and dispose of the pads in an approved manner.

net works surprising well) and mix it into the used motor oil from changing the oil in my truck. This I dispose of through my place of employment. You will have to find where in your community used oil can be properly disposed of. If you need to dump the water after just one testing session, I would suggest allowing the water to sit for a few hours (a day or two would be better) and then sopping up the oil and gasoline that will rise to the surface with an oil-absorbing pad that you can buy at good auto parts stores. Then the water can be dumped in good conscience (although if it flows into a sewer or stream of some sort, it still may not be legal). A review of your local pollution laws is probably in order.

Back to trouble-shooting. If your outboard does not run, or does not run correctly, the most important tool to have is an analytical mind—the ability to logically determine what the problem is without introducing assump-

Figure 16-04
A 1953 25 HP Big Twin goes bucket cruising after an ignition tune-up which included new condensers. I failed to get the wire to one condenser tucked-in properly and the flywheel cut the wire, killing the engine. Replacing the condenser with another new one was not a big deal, and since the problem was discovered at home, a day of boating was not lost.

tions or drawing unsubstantiated conclusions. In simple terms, take your time and think about exactly what the outboard is doing and is not doing, and don't assume anything.

Did the outboard run before your repaired or changed something on it? Chances are the problem arose with that repair or change. This is a good reason why I suggest for the novice,

Figure 16-05
The Big Twin doing its thing. Working on old outboards is not rocket science, guys; you can learn to do it if you want to and if you put your mind to it.

(once he has his outboard running for the first time), only repair one item at a time and test run before moving on to the next item. If the outboard ran before your cleaned the carburetor and does not run afterwards it is logical to assume that the carb or some aspect of its installation (such as fuel hoses or gaskets) is the problem. If you cleaned the carb, installed a new fuel pump, installed new points and condensers and spark plug wires, and the engine does not run afterwards, trouble-shooting is more complicated. Of course, I suggest your doing all of this sort of work on an engine you have just acquired unless you have seen it run. At that point you are starting from "zero," and tending to these items can actually reduce the amount of trouble shooting that you need to do.

A trait of the good trouble shooting is observing details: If the engine was running and then just quit as if the ignition was shut off, maybe the ignition *was* shut off and you need to look at the magneto and related wiring, including a stop switch if the engine has one.

Remove the spark plugs and have a good look at their electrodes. If the plugs do not look the same (one plug fouled with black carbon or wet with fuel mixture) there is a good chance that the problem is in the ignition system. If you attach the plugs to the plug wires and ground the outer metal shell of the plug to some bare metal of the engine, does the plug give a "snappy" blue spark when you spin the engine? Do both plugs spark? If not, switch the plugs to see if that makes any difference. See if you can isolate the problem to a bad spark plug, or does using a new plug make no difference? Did the points gap go out of adjustment? Or did a drop of oil contaminate the points?

Of course, plugs that look the same do not totally eliminate the ignition system from suspicion, but if the porcelain ends of both plugs are a nice light brown color and both plugs give a good blue audible spark, chances are the ignition system is okay and you can move on the fuel system.

Obviously, the engine needs gasoline to run. The gasoline has to make it into the carburetor and then be mixed with the proper amount of air. Is gasoline getting to the carburetor? Is there a glass sediment bowl (most of the old OMCs had them) that looks like it is full of crud or water? Is there any gasoline actually making it as far as the sediment bowl? Is there water in your gasoline? Did you try using a different fuel tank?

If you disconnect the fuel hose from the carburetor and use the primer bulb or primer pump does fuel flow from that hose? If not, work your way back through the system until you have fuel and you have isolated the problem.

A fuel-pump-equipped motor that acts like it is running out of fuel even through the fuel tank is full may have a vacuum leak somewhere between the fuel tank and the fuel pump. The most likely spots are the O-ring seals at the quick connectors in the fuel hose. But it could also be a hole in a fuel line or primer bulb. See any gas leakage anywhere? What about the strainer on the bottom of the fuel pick-up tube in the remote fuel tank? Is it clean?

If your outboard is overheating, how old is the pump impeller? Did you run the engine in sand or extremely dirty/gritty water lately? If you just installed a new impeller and the engine overheats, did you get the water tube installed correctly when mounting the lower unit? Did the rubber grommet that seals the water tube to the pump body get damaged while installing the lower unit? For those models with a thermostat, is it stuck closed?

There are many things that can cause an outboard to run improperly or not run at all. Trouble-shooting is the methodical elimination of items that are right, and which will eventually present you with what is wrong. Care in choosing an outboard that is not heavily damaged due to neglect or abuse can go a long way towards reducing the potential for problems, and carefully studying parts diagrams and service manuals can help you keep from creating your own problems. The factory did not sell any outboards that would not run. So you just need to figure out what is different about it now that causes it not to run.

Now that you have your head screwed on right, consult the trouble-shooting charts that nearly all service manuals (even the generic ones) have. Resign yourself to working through the problem in a logical methodical way. If you get frustrated, walk away from the outboard for an hour, or a day or more, if necessary. Have a seat in the "moaning chair" that I mentioned way back in the introduction. Better yet, take the wife out to dinner, the kids out to a show, or the girlfriend out dancing (don't *even* tell me you have all three!). Let the motor sit for a while and give yourself a chance to think things over. The problem that seems so big at the moment may shrink with time.

I think you can do it.

I figured it all out, and I really doubt I am any smarter than you are.

17

Onboard Spares and Tools

I like to say that modern outboard motors are "fool-proof," while older outboards are motors that "any fool can fix." You can't deal with mechanical problems on the water, however, if you do not have some basic tools and maybe some spare parts in the boat.

The tools and spares that I carry in the boat will vary depending upon the circumstances. For example, if I am based out of a campground, where cruises will be short and in the immediate area, I see little need to carry other than maybe a spare shear pin or two (see propellers chapter) along with the tools necessary to install them. Usually, a large pair of pliers will remove the cotter pin and propeller nut, although an adjustable wrench might be kinder on the "flats" of a threaded prop nut. With other boats nearby, there is little chance of a breakdown leaving you in dire straits. The 14-foot 1956 aluminum Crestliner boat that I take to antique outboard motor meets usually represents this level of preparedness. You can be sure that I will have tools and maybe some spares in my pickup truck, but I will carry little in the boat on the short ten or fifteen minutes excursions that are the usual activities at

these meets. I might also carry a spare propeller, but that is about it.

Those familiar with the function of a shear pin might question the necessity of carrying a spare propeller, but as someone who has had the rubber cushioned hub of a propeller fail, allowing the blades to spin freely on the hub, I think it wise to carry the prop. Having two props also allows you to have both "speed" (high pitch) and "power" (low pitch) props to use with different loads.

The other extreme of preparedness is when you are traveling long distances through remote areas or without the company of other boats. In these circumstances, more tools and spares are called for, and I generally keep my Jim Michalak-designed home-built 18-foot cabin skiff stocked to this level of preparedness. I have a full set of wrenches and sockets, an adjustable (crescent) wrench, several screwdrivers; regular, needlenose, and locking (Vise-Grip) pliers and a few other miscellaneous tools. I suppose that I

Figure 17-01
This is the tool and spares kit that I carry onboard my 18-foot cabin skiff. Everything fits inside a plastic container that is kept underneath the spashwell at the stern. This particular container makes better use of the space available than a typical tool box would.

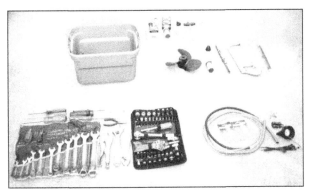

Figure 17-02
You can fit quite a bit of stuff into these plastic containers.

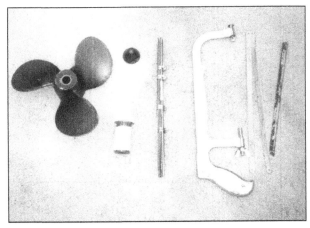

Figure 17-03
Spare propeller and propeller nut, with shear pins and cotter pins in the pill jar. In the center of the photo are several lengths of brass rod of varying diameters. The hacksaw can be used to cut shear pins of any length needed from the brass rods. Since I often run different engines, the rods and saw allow me to custom-cut a shear pin for just about any old OMC outboard. If you have but a single engine, all you need to carry is a few pins that will fit your engine. Note the worm-screw hose clamps binding the rods together; it is sometimes handy to have a few extra clamps onboard.

should mention that the tools carried should be in SAE (Society of Automotive Engineers) "inch" sizes and not metric (Figure 17-01).

Spare parts kept aboard the cabin skiff consist of a propeller, propeller nut, cotter pins, shear pins, a couple of sparkplugs, a few short lengths of different size fuel hose and a couple of spare "in-line" fuel filters, and a water pump impeller. One advantage of the older OMC engines is the interchangeability of some replacement parts; for example, the pump impeller that I carry fits both the 1957 Johnson 18 HP that I usually run on the skiff, along with the 1956 Johnson 10 that I use on the boat on lakes with 10 HP limits. The spark plugs also fit both of those engines and also the 1955 Johnson 5½ HP engine that serves as an auxiliary engine. The pump impeller, however, will not fit the 5½.

That 5½ is sort of a "spare" as well. I have never had to use the spare engine to get to where I was going but I still like to carry it on the skiff, which is fitted with a lifting bracket for it. The 5½, replaced a 3 HP that really did not have the power to handle the 18-foot skiff in wind or current. Also, the main engines use pressurized remote fuel tanks (see fuel tank chapter) as does the 5½, whereas the 3 HP used

an engine-mounted, gravity-fed fuel tank that required me to carry a small portable gas can for refueling it. The 5½ can be run with the main tanks.

The Crestliner is not set up for a spare engine, but then I rarely travel far from "home base" in that boat. I always carry a paddle in both boats, and once I used the paddle in the Crestliner to good advantage when I "blew up" the 1940 Johnson I was running that day. I was upwind of the dock and not too far out and managed to "sail" back to the marina using the paddle to steer and to control leeway.

As previously mentioned, most of the engines I run use pressurized remote fuel tanks, and each tank has its own fuel hose perma-

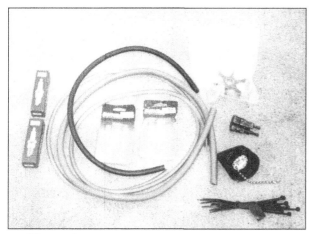

Figure 17-04
A couple of spark plugs, some fuel hose in different diameters, a pair of "in-line" fuel filters (which I use on all of my old outboards), and a water pump impeller. Also shown is a spare cap for a pressurized remote fuel tank (the tank isn't going to hold pressure if you lose the cap overboard) along with a spare hose quick connector for a pressure tank. The wire ties sometimes come in handy for "jury-rigged" repairs.

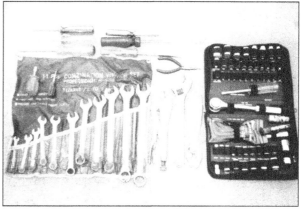

Figure 17-05
A cheap set of "combination" (open-end and box-end) wrenches in SAE sizes, screwdrivers in both regular and Phillips types, with several sizes of each, and a small set of socket wrenches. Pliers in "regular," locking, and needlenose varieties, and an adjustable (crescent) wrench. That's a set of "feeler" gauges next to the needle-nose pliers, for setting spark plug gaps and ignition point gaps.

nently mounted. Remote tanks for outboards equipped with fuel pumps often have a quick connector at both the outboard and also on the remote tank, allowing one fuel hose to be used with two or more tanks. I will not leave the dock for all but the shortest cruises on the friendliest of waters without at least two fuel hoses on board, even if I only have one remote tank. The fuel hose assembly is easy to damage, especially the primer bulb of fuel hoses for fuel pump-equipped engines. I have had O-rings in quick connectors tear, destroying the seal and preventing the fuel pump from drawing fuel from the tank. Countless rubber fuel hoses have been cut by bouncing tackle boxes, deck chairs, and other gear. Since the hoses are permanently clamped to pressure tanks, I prefer to carry two small tanks rather than one big tank,

which not only provides redundant hoses but also redundant tanks, as old pressure tanks, inherently more complicated than fuel pump tanks, are a bit more prone to problems.

A word about spark plug fouling, where the inner end of the spark plug becomes so caked with carbon and other crap that it doesn't spark anymore, and the engine doesn't run anymore. Decades ago, this was a common problem with outboards. Fouled plugs rarely occur today, as modern 2-cycle oils burn very cleanly and leave few deposits behind. I have not fouled a spark plug since 1994, although I do make a habit of replacing the plugs every year or two, whether they need to be replaced or not. It is still a good idea to carry spare plugs however on the longer trips. Although a fouled plug can be removed from the engine, cleaned, and reinstalled, you would be surprised by the number of cleaned plugs that accidentally end up dropped into the deep. Although most spark plugs can be removed and installed with the adjustable wrench, be sure to check your engine. A deep spark plug socket wrench might be required if there is little clearance around the plugs.

A final note: A person who has resurrected an old outboard purchased at a garage sale or flea market will have an advantage on the water if and when trouble occurs over a person who has never cleaned the carburetor or replaced the fuel lines or adjusted the points on his outboard. Being familiar with your engine can eliminate much of the mystery of dealing with engine problems on the water.

A little practical mechanical experience can be the most useful "tool" you can possess on a boat.

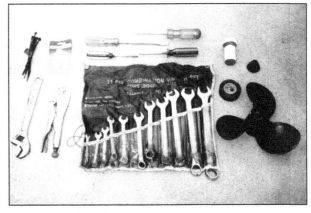

Figure 17-07
My suggested tool kit for anyone running a 1950s or 1960s OMC outboard: a set of combination wrenches, an adjustable wrench, locking pliers, two different sizes of both regular and Phillips screwdrivers, electrical tape, spare fuel filter (if your engine uses one—and it should), and spare prop., prop nut, shear pins and cotter pins. It would not hurt to add a set of spark plugs to the kit as well.

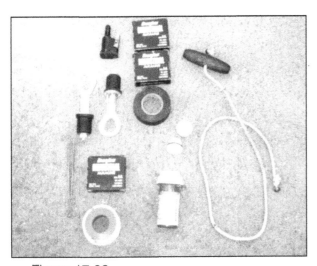

Figure 17-06
Misc. items: spare boat plugs in the two different sizes used on my cabin skiff: extra batteries (AA size) for the little flashlights that I have onboard, a starter rope to be used if the recoil starter on an outboard fails, electrical tape, teflon plumber's tape (used to seal the threads on the cheap plastic garboard drain plugs I installed on the boat), and a pill bottle containing some spare hardware for the bimini top.

Figure 17-08
The ultimate spare: a complete second engine. Of course, it adds weight, takes up space, and is an added expense. Sometimes comes in handy for trolling.

APPENDIX

TORQUE SPECIFICATIONS - SCREWS, NUTS, BOLTS & STUDS

(Refer to the Evinrude Service Manual for torques on engines not listed)

Proper tightening of screws, nuts, etc., is vitally important in properly servicing Evinrude engines just as it is for any other machinery.

Pulling screws down too tightly may result in stripped threads which increase labor costs to drill, tap and install heli-coils. Leaving a screw too loose may allow vibration to back it completely out. In some cases, such screws may get into moving parts of the powerhead or gearcase and cause damage to the engine.

GENERAL TORQUE SPECIFICATIONS:
These apply to all engines unless otherwise specified under the individual engine specifications.

SCREW SIZE:	Ft. Lbs.	Inch Lbs.
#6 (32 & 40 thds.)	-	7-10
#10 (24 & 32 ")	2-3	24-36
#12 (24 & 28 ")	3-4	36-48
¼" (20 & 28 ")	5-7	60-84
5/16" (18 & 24 thds.)	10-12	120-144
3/8" (16 & 24 ")	18-20	216-240
Spark plugs (all models)	20-20½	240-246

MISCELLANEOUS		
Diodes (AC generator)	15	180
Bendix drive nut (starter)	20-25	240-300

The only recommended method for properly tightening screws is by using a torque wrench. Torque wrenches may be purchased at reasonable cost and will rapidly pay for themselves in quality service work.

TORQUE IN FOOT POUNDS EXCEPT AS SPECIFIED

1960 THRU 1964 MODELS	3 HP	5½ HP	9½ HP	10 HP	18 HP	28 - 40 HP	60 - 75 - 90 HP
POWERHEAD (screws, nuts or bolts):							
By-pass cover				2-3*	5-7*	5-7*	4-7*
...Cut out switch adapter to by-pass cover						12-13 in. lbs.	
Connecting rod	5-5½*	5-5½*	8*	15-15½	15-15½	29-31	29-31
Crankcase to cylinder-all bearings	5-7*	5-7*	10-12	10-12	10-12	13½-14	13½-14
Crankcase head - top & bottom							8-10
Cylinder head	5-7*	5-7*	8-10	8-10	8-10	14-16	14-16
Cylinder head cover							3-7*
Exhaust cover	2-3*	2-3*		2-3*	5-7*	5-7*	5-7*
Filler block-crankshaft							14-16
Flywheel nut	30-40	40-45	40-45	40-45	40-45	100-105	70-85
Flywheel to ring or ring gear					12-14	12-14	12-14
Generator mounting bracket						5-7*	
Generator mounting nuts						5-7*	
Intake manifold	2-3*	2-3*		2-3*	5-7*	2-3*	5-7*
Safety (micro) switch mounting						7-10 in. lbs.	7-10 in. lbs.
Starter mounting bracket-electric						5-7*	
Starter mounting-manual	3-5*	8-10		8-10	8-10	8-10	8-10
...Starter mounting-manual-rear						14-16	
Starter ratchet to flywheel						6-8*	
Thermostat cover to cylinder head		3-5*		3-5*	3-5*	5-7*	
Thermostat housing							3½-4½*
Thermostat housing to adaptor							2-4*
Heat exchanger to exhaust cover						18-20	18-20
LOWER UNIT (screws, nuts or bolts):							
Gearcase to exhaust tube (& 5" ext.)	5-7*	5-7*	5-7*	5-7*	5-7*	10-12	16-18
Gearcase to exhaust housing-rear					18-20	18-20	
Gearcase studs						28-32	21-28
Gearcase stud nuts						24-26	24-26
Lever to shift rod clamp		4-5*		4-5*	4-5*	4-5*	4-5*
Lower mount housing to pilot shaft		6-8*		6-8*	14-16		
Rubber mount-front-upper		12-14		12-14	12-14	20-26	18-20
Rubber mount-side-upper & lower		12-14		12-14	12-14	12-14	10-12
Rubber mount-lower motor cover				6-8*	6-8*		
Oil & drain plugs	5-7	5-7	5-7	5-7	5-7	5-7	5-7
Skeg to upper gearcase		5-7*		5-7*	5-7*	5-7*	
Steering bracket to pilot shaft		5-7*		5-7*	5-7*	10-12	
Set Screws**-gear to clutch spring						15-20 in. lbs.	15-20 in. lbs.

*Use Inch Pounds for greater accuracy. Multiply indicated Foot Pounds by 12. Use torque wrench calibrated in Inch Pounds.
**Clean oil from parts with cleaning solvent. Allow to dry. Apply one drop "Loctite," grade "D," to threads of each screw.

Although these torque figures are specific to 1960 model year outboards, other model years will be similar with the exception that torque figures listed for 40 hp flywheel nuts are for 1960 and 1961 only.

About the Author

Introduced to the Mississippi River and to boats at a young age by his parents, Max E. Wawrzyniak III has never strayed far from the water. After high school graduation, he took a job as a deckhand aboard Mississippi River towboats for a year and a half before attending college (and earning a totally useless B.A. in English.) Post-college found him back on the Mississippi River where he eventually moved from the deck to the pilothouse, spending several years as a pilot of commercial towing vessels and passenger vessels. Additional college courses in accounting and succesful completion of the examination for Certified Public Accountant preceded a career move to "land-side," where for the last sixteen years he has "crunched numbers" in the riverside office of a major Mississippi River barge line with only an occasional wistful gaze at the Mississippi flowing endlessly by outside of the windows.

A life-long pleasure boater, a "bean-counter" instinct for economical boating lead him to old outboard motors more than a decade ago and he is currently the owner of about 150 outboard motors, dating from 1918 to 1979. A graduate of the School of Hard Knocks, Old Outboard Motor curriculum (with an advanced degree in knuckle-busting from the University of Adversity) Max is a self-taught old-outboard-motor mechanic, if you don't include the multitudes of friends and outboard collectors who have helped him along the way.

The search for inexpensive boats to run his old outboards on lead Max to small craft designer Jim Michalak, author of *Boatbuilding for Beginners (and Beyond)*, and Jim's easy-to-build boat plans. To date Max has completed four of Jim's designs.

In 2003 however, at 250 pounds and gaining, it became obvious to Max that he might not have enough time left in order to "mess" with all of those old outboards if changes weren't made, so he got his eating under control and began walking 5 to 6 miles each day which eventually evolved into runnning 6 to 8 miles each day. Now weighing 147 pounds, Max has run a 5K and a 10-mile race and also a half-marathon. He would like to eventually run a full marathon if he can find the time between working on old outboards, building wooden boats, and making a living.

Other boating titles from Breakaway Books

Available in bookstores and most as e-books, too.

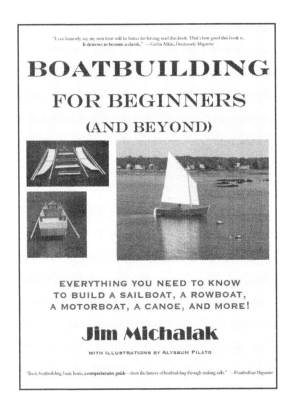

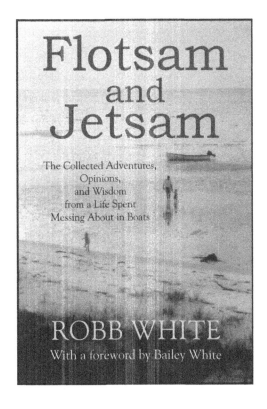

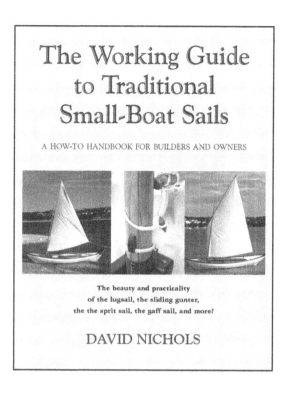

The Working Guide to Traditional Small-Boat Sails

A HOW-TO HANDBOOK FOR BUILDERS AND OWNERS

The beauty and practicality
of the lugsail, the sliding gunter,
the the sprit sail, the gaff sail, and more!

DAVID NICHOLS

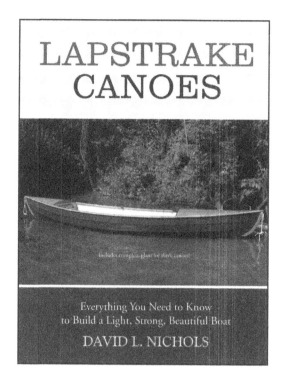

LAPSTRAKE CANOES

Includes complete plans for three canoes!

Everything You Need to Know
to Build a Light, Strong, Beautiful Boat

DAVID L. NICHOLS

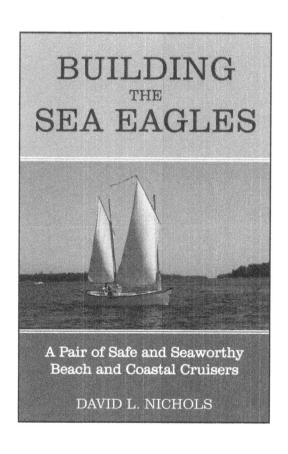

BUILDING
THE
SEA EAGLES

A Pair of Safe and Seaworthy
Beach and Coastal Cruisers

DAVID L. NICHOLS

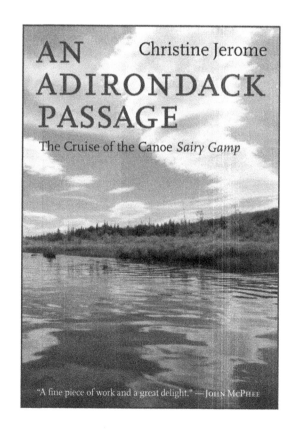

Christine Jerome

AN ADIRONDACK PASSAGE

The Cruise of the Canoe *Sairy Gamp*

"A fine piece of work and a great delight." —JOHN MCPHEE

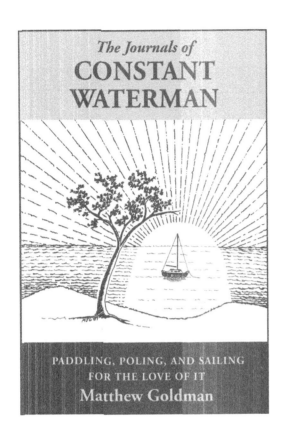

The Journals of
CONSTANT WATERMAN

PADDLING, POLING, AND SAILING
FOR THE LOVE OF IT

Matthew Goldman

Moon Wind
at Large

SAILING HITHER AND YON

Written and illustrated by
Constant Waterman
(aka Matthew Goldman)